P R A I S E F

The depth of Soul Survivor's experience in youth ministry is finally available for youth groups everywhere! Soul Survivor Encounter utilizes the gospel to energize your students, impassion your leaders and immerse your community in the values of service, relationship, worship, justice and evangelism. Don't miss out on this series of truly fantastic resources!

Josh McDowell
Speaker
Author, *Evidence That Demands a Verdict*

Soul Survivor is undoubtedly in the center of this generation's fresh wind of the Spirit. The message is clear and spiritually motivating. This material is wonderful.

Jim Burns
Founder and President, YouthBuilders

When a devotional starts with quotes from Beyoncé, Jessica Simpson or Clint Eastwood, something's up. In the case of Soul Survivor Encounter, that something is starting with youths' real lives, not with a religious subculture. A refreshing mix of classical theology with feet firmly planted in the neighborhood.

Sally Morgenthaler
Speaker
Founder, Sacramentis.com and Digital Glass Videos

There is no greater challenge facing us today than to engage emerging generations with the truths of the Scriptures, and Soul Survivor Encounter hits the bull's-eye in how to go about doing that.

Dan Kimball
Author, *The Emerging Church: Vintage Christianity for New Generations*
Pastor, Vintage Faith Church, Santa Cruz, California

Soul Survivor is a win-win resource. Youth leaders win with user-friendly resources that bring depth to their ministries. Students win with engaging discussion and reflection tools that help connect the dots between their faith and their life.

Kara Powell
Executive Director, Fuller Seminary Center
for Ministry to Youth and Their Families

From the start, Soul Survivor Encounter grabs you and doesn't let go. This new series of materials for students is grounded in the Bible, in touch with the world, full of activities and ideas; a truly interactive thrill for students and their youth leaders!

Darlene Zschech
Worship Leader

Soul Survivor Encounter hits kids where they are on several levels. It is culturally current, interactive, community building and solidly biblical. It brings God's Word right into the teenage world with personal stories, practical application and action steps. It moves from information to transformation and is hip without being flip. With journaling, projects and daily devotions, the Christian life becomes whole, rather than an isolated Sunday experience. Most of all Jesus, the eternal Son of God, is presented as the compelling Lord to be worshiped and a friend to share life with 24/7.

Don Williams, Ph.D.
Speaker
Author, *Twelve Steps with Jesus*

soulsurvivor

leader'sguide

LIVING THE LIFE
SURVIVORS

Gospel Light

PUBLISHED BY GOSPEL LIGHT
VENTURA, CALIFORNIA, U.S.A.
PRINTED IN THE U.S.A.

Gospel Light is a Christian publisher dedicated to serving the local church. We believe God's vision for Gospel Light is to provide church leaders with biblical, user-friendly materials that will help them evangelize, disciple and minister to children, youth and families.

It is our prayer that this Gospel Light resource will help you discover biblical truth for your own life and help you minister to youth. May God richly bless you.

For a free catalog of resources from Gospel Light, please contact your Christian supplier or contact us at 1-800-4-GOSPEL or www.gospellight.com.

PUBLISHING STAFF

William T. Greig, Chairman · **Dr. Elmer L. Towns,** Senior Consulting Publisher · **Alex Field,** Associate Editor · **Bayard Taylor, M.Div.,** Senior Editor, Biblical and Theological Issues · **Mike Pilavachi,** General Editor · **Tom Stephen, Virginia Starkey, Marcus Brotherton,** Contributors · **Samantha Hsu,** Art Director · **Rosanne Moreland,** Designer

ISBN 0-8307-3655-7
© 2004 Gospel Light
All rights reserved.
Printed in the U.S.A.

contents

How to Use the Student Magazine

GETTING STARTED

All leader's notes, tips and activities that do not appear in the student magazine will appear in shaded areas. In completing the student magazine, you might have your students work on each session prior to a youth-group or small-group meeting, during which you can cover the material in more depth.

Every student magazine breaks down into sections that students can complete by themselves and in large or small groups. During your journey through the Soul Survivor Encounter, you and your students will find the following headings:

status

Each session begins with quotations and interview excerpts under the Status heading. For more quotations and complete interviews, visit www.SoulSurvivorEncounter.com. **Note:** The Status section features quotations from Christians, celebrities and pop culture personalities that address key issues. The purpose of these quotations is to acknowledge a variety of worldviews so that students and leaders can enter into a frank discussion of about each one. The quotations are conversation starters that provoke thought and discussion, challenging students to hold each quotation up to the light of Scripture in the pages that follow each Status section.

the story

The Story contains the session's key issues. Students may also read a few verses from the Bible and hear stories that are key in understanding the session's topic.

break it down

In Break It Down, students focus on the main points again by working on an individual creative project or activity.

comeback

In Comeback, students meet in small groups to share thoughts on the topic and activities they completed in the Story and Break It Down sections.

project revolution

The Project Revolution suggestions guide students in planning a project that they can do as a group or on their own. Their projects should be completed outside the church walls.

momentum

This section challenges students to go deeper in Scripture. Check out Time in the Word—a five-day devotional. The Momentum section on the Soul Survivor Encounter website features further study options as well (see www.SoulSurvivorEncounter.com).

preface

Ten years ago, Soul Survivor began in a little youth ministry at an Anglican church in a village called Chorleywood, outside of London. The heart of Soul Survivor is to encourage, equip, recruit, train and release young people into ministry.

I was an accountant until I was 29 years old; then God rescued me. He set me free and delivered me from the bondage of Egypt. One day the vicar of my Anglican church called me—he'd never done that before. He said, "Can you come and see me this evening?" And I thought, *Oh, my goodness, he's discovered some of my secret sins and I'm going to get rebuked*. I was really nervous, repenting and dealing with my issues.

I went to his house that evening, and to my relief, he hadn't discovered any of my secret sins. Instead, he wanted to give me the job as youth pastor. So I quickly said, "Yes," before he discovered my secret sins and changed his mind.

When I started as the youth pastor of this church, I wanted to be the best. I hit the ground running, organizing concerts, and young people from the whole area came out to see some of the best Christian bands in England, at least at that time.

You probably haven't heard of these bands because it was a generation ago. We had groups like Martin Joseph, Phil and John, and Fat and Frantic. There was actually a band called Fat and Frantic, and they were amazing. They actually wrote a song called "Last Night My Wife Hoovered My Head." I mean, it just says everything, doesn't it? It's wonderful.

Anyway, we filled the place with young people, and I thought, *Yes, I'm a success. Yes, look at all these young people*. But somewhere in the midst of that, I started to have this sinking feeling that all was not well. I realized that as more and more young people came to the gatherings and the events, our own youth group was shrinking. Then, after a couple of incidents, I realized that something was very wrong.

One night I decided to have a video evening. I got a film out and mounted these big TV monitors on the walls of the church lounge and hooked them up to a VCR. I blacked out the windows, and I bought—with my own money—popcorn, chips, peanuts and stuff like that. I put them in little bowls between the armchairs and got out sodas and drinks. I couldn't have done more if I had put on a frilly white dress and walked up and down the aisles during the intermission selling ice cream.

At the beginning of the evening the students arrived and sat down. I did a little stand-up comedy routine, and then we showed the main feature. As we did that, they had their popcorn, chips and peanuts, and they drank their sodas and drinks.

At the end of the evening, they all started to leave. As they walked out, I looked around, and I thought, *Oh, my goodness, this is a bomb site*. In this room, there were crushed peanuts, chips and popcorn on the carpet. There was even soda dripping from the walls and the tables. As I looked around, my heart sank. One of the last to leave was a girl named Emma, and she came up to me, folded her arms and said, "Mike, this room is a mess." And I thought, *Thank you for your discernment*. Then she said "You're going to have to get a Hoover to clean this," and she left. They all had left. They had left me to clean up their rubbish.

As I cleaned up their rubbish, I got more and more angry. As I vacuumed the carpet and washed the walls, I thought to myself, *These young people, they're not Christians. They're not disciples. They're consumers. All they ever do is take, take, take. They just consume everything. They don't have a disciple's bone in their bodies*. And I thought, *Right, from now on, every week, studies in Leviticus. I'll show them. That's the last time they get a band. That's the last time they get a video*.

I was so mad. Then, suddenly, in the midst of all that, this thought came into my mind: *And who made them like that*? You know what, I didn't need a sermon at that point because I knew that I'd made them like that. I'd made our relationship that of provider and client, and they'd done their job of being consumers brilliantly.

So I realized that I had a problem. By trying to entertain young people into the kingdom of God, I would have to spend the rest of my life entertaining them to keep them there. It wasn't working. Then I read this little book on how

Jesus discipled the disciples. I discovered that Jesus' method was very different from mine. I discovered how Jesus got beside them, and He did stuff with them and through them and then He sent them out.

There was a time when He sent them out in pairs to heal the sick and cast out demons. One time the disciples came across a boy possessed by a demon, but they couldn't cast it out. So they asked Jesus, "Oh, Lord, oh, Lord, why couldn't we cast out the demon?" And then Jesus said, and I'm going to paraphrase slightly here, "Well, good try, guys. It's good that you tried, but it didn't come out because you have too little faith" (see Matthew 17:19-20).

Now, after He said that, do you think they remembered that lesson? Do you think they remembered it better than if they'd gone to a daylong seminar on casting out demons and point *F* was, "This kind of demon comes out by faith"? I think they remembered that lesson because they had experienced failure.

Another time they came back, and they were like, "Oh, Lord, you should have been there. It was an amazing ministry trip! Even the demons flee when we tell them to leave in Your name" (see Luke 10:17).

And then Jesus said, "So you remembered the lesson about faith, huh?"

They probably replied, "Oh, yeah, faith—we remembered that."

Then He said, "Well done, guys, you sorted out that demon. I saw Satan fall like lightning from the sky and that suggests he didn't like what happened. But rejoice not that the demons flee; rejoice rather that your names are written in the book of life" (see Luke 10:18-20).

It was like He said, "You learned the faith lesson, now here's the next one: humility and the big picture." Jesus did that with them all the time.

That's how discipleship happens. We have to make space in our churches and in our ministries to allow people to mess up brilliantly. We need to devote ourselves to encouraging, affirming and reaching out to the next generation.

I long for us to seek Him for the next generation in so many different ways. To find ways of cheering them on so that they might be all they can be. To find ways of cheering them on so that they can be all they can be for the sake of the Lord and for the sake of the lost.

Mike Pilavachi
Ventura, CA
May 28, 2003

living
the life

Is "Evangelism" a Dirty Word?

Note: All leader's options and tips are in shaded areas.

before everyone shows up

1. Pray for the students who will attend this study. Ask the Holy Spirit to guide you as a teacher and the students as they learn.
2. Work through the entire session on your own and mark the areas that you want to focus on during the study. If you have a student leadership team, consider assigning various portions of the study to student leaders to lead, but give them time to prepare.
3. **Optional Student Assignment:** Give the students the study a week ahead of time so that they can complete it before they come to the first session.
4. Watch for relevant celebrity quotations and news stories that could be used to discuss evangelism. You can use these during the Status section. Check out www.SoulSurvivorEncounter.com for more stories and quotations.
5. Gather the needed supplies and make sure that all technology is working.
6. View the corresponding Soul Survivor video segment ahead of time.
7. Create a welcoming environment with music and light refreshments. You may also want to ask different students or their parents to bring snacks each week. An adult volunteer or student leader could be in charge of coordinating this aspect of the meeting each week.

GETTING STARTED

1. When the students arrive, greet them and learn names you don't know.
2. Pray for God's guidance as you begin the study.
3. Ask the students if they would like to read the Bible passages during the study. If anyone volunteers, give him or her a sheet with the passages written on it. Be sensitive to those who may not like to read out loud.

Icebreakers

Option 1: Divide the students into groups of two students each and have each person answer the following questions:

1. What do you most like to do on a Saturday morning?

2. What movie did you most recently see that was not worth the price of admission?

3. What do you most dislike about people's sharing their faith?

4. Who do you most respect as a person with integrity?

After the small groups have time to talk, have each student introduce his or her partner to the group by sharing his or her partner's answers to any two of the four questions.

Option 2: Set out a wide variety of colored paper and ask each student to choose the color that he or she thinks best represents either how he or she feels about his or her day or how he or she feels about telling people about God. Have students tell why they chose the color they chose.

status

Read through the quotations and interview excerpt as a group. Also, if you collected any other quotations or news stories, share those. Invite the students to comment on the quotation that strikes them as being the most interesting.

Tip: The Soul Survivor website, www.Soul Survivor Encounter.com, is updated periodically with quotations, interviews, icebreakers and more.

WHAT PEOPLE ARE SAYING

JIM BAKKER, FORMER TELEVANGELIST

In referring to his luxury religious center, Heritage USA, Bakker said, "Why should I apologize because God throws in crystal chandeliers, mahogany doors, and the best construction in the world?"[1]

KENT SHARKEY, TECHNICAL EVANGELIST

In an interview, Sharkey, .NET Compact Framework Technical Evangelist for Microsoft, described his job: "The Technical Evangelist role is always good for a smile. There aren't too many companies willing to call people that. Basically, our role is to go forth into the community to introduce developers to technologies that aren't shipping yet. We are the advance scouts, if you will, preparing people for changes to come."[2]

MEL GIBSON, ACTOR

"My hope is that [*The Passion of the Christ*] will affect people on a very profound level and reach them with a message of faith, hope, love and forgiveness."[3]

MAHATMA GANDHI, ACTIVIST

"It is a first class human tragedy that people of the earth who claim to believe in the message of Jesus, whom they describe as the Prince of Peace, show little of that belief in actual practice."[4]

INTERVIEW

Subject: Vicky Beeching, Soul Survivor worship leader
Soul Survivor: When did you first truly meet or experience God?
Vicky Beeching: When I was seven, my mum asked me if I wanted to give my life to Jesus. We'd been talking a lot about who Jesus was over the years, and I knew I wanted to make that commitment. Kneeling down in our family room, she led me through a little prayer, and I remember not being able to hold back the tears. Now I know that feeling was God's presence and His Holy Spirit, but I think that was one of the first times I strongly experienced Him like that.

See the rest of this interview and more thought-provoking quotes at www.SoulSurvivorEncounter.com.

After reading this section together, ask the students if they have heard other stories during the week that have to do with evangelism. Encourage students to watch for what celebrities or their friends might say about next week's topic, which is Soul to Soul, or relationships.

video segment

Show the corresponding Soul Survivor video clip on the *Living the Life & Survivors* DVD. **Option 1:** Before the students watch the video, give each student a piece of paper and a pencil or pen, and as the students watch the video, have them write down their thoughts and feelings about what is said.

Option 2: Watch a scene from the movie *Leap of Faith* (Paramount Studios, 1992). After watching a scene of your choice, ask the students to give their impressions of an evangelist. How does Steve Martin's character demonstrate a twisted view of Christians? If you have time, watch the final scene to show how even corrupt people can encounter the living God.

Have you ever entered a store and found the salesperson smiling big, acting like your best friend and then trying to convince you to buy something you didn't want? In this situation, you are being used—to the salesperson, you're just another sale. But the truth is that nobody likes to be used.

Unfortunately, when it comes to sharing our faith, many Christians use others to get what they want: money, converts or a bigger youth group. We see preachers on television and it seems like they just want our money. Strangers knock on the door and feign interest in you, but they just want you to join their church.

Merriam-Webster's Collegiate Dictionary defines "evangelism" as "militant or crusading zeal,"[5] but who wants to be the object of someone's crusading zeal? For many in the world, "evangelism" is a dirty word.

We may think, *I don't want others to force their beliefs on me, so why should I force my beliefs on others?* The answer is that God never intended for us to be militant when we share our faith. God simply wants us to show people His love.

A NEW LOOK AT EVANGELISM

Jesus was not the first in His extended family to become a preacher or an evangelist. John the Baptist, Jesus' first cousin, started preaching before Jesus began His ministry. The ordinary people loved John, while religious leaders thought John was a troublemaker, even though he told the truth. In fact, John was thrown into prison because of his preaching.

While in prison, John began to question whether Jesus was the Messiah. He wanted proof that God had sent Jesus to Earth.

Jesus replied, "Go back and report to John what you hear and see: The blind receive sight, the lame walk, those who have leprosy are cured, the deaf hear, the dead are raised, and the good news is preached to the poor. Blessed is the man who does not fall away on account of me" (Matthew 11:4-6).

Is Jesus' approach to sharing God's love as outlined in Matthew 11:4-6, different from what we typically call evangelism?

MONEY OR THE ABILITY TO WALK

After His resurrection, Jesus spent time instructing His disciples. In Acts 1, Jesus actually describes for His disciples what they should do: "But you will receive power when the Holy Spirit comes on you; and you will be my witnesses in Jerusalem, and in all Judea and Samaria, and to the ends of the earth" (v. 8).

How did the disciples proclaim the good news? They did what Jesus did. They preached and met people's needs. One of the first stories of evangelism comes in Acts 3. Peter and John are walking to church and see a man who can't walk begging for money. In fact, the man had never been able to walk.

How would most people react to this man? Would they give him money? Ignore him? Pray for him? Would they command him to stand up and walk?

Action

Read Acts 3. How do you think the healed man would describe Peter and John's evangelism technique? How can Christians today meet people's needs to demonstrate God's love?

break it down

Take some time now to find your own personal space to work on this activity. If you can, go back to the same space each week to complete this section. Finally, ponder the following and then complete the action step.

- You are here today because somebody told you about God's love.
- You are here today because someone demonstrated that God cares for your needs.
- Can you think of a positive image of evangelism or a person who shared the love of God with you?

Action

Now write a list poem to describe how you've experienced a positive image of evangelism. List words or phrases that could complete the sentence below. Also list the name or names of people that come to mind.

_____ helped me to understand
(name of person)   God's love by . . .

comeback

Have students form small groups. You may want to decide ahead of time whether you would like them to have the same small group for the length of the study. The personalities of your group will help inform your decision. After each student shares his or her poem, ask the students to work through the questions below.

Now form small groups to read your list poems to one another. If you are working alone, find a friend to share how you sense God speaking to you through the study. Then discuss the following questions together:

- How do the images in your poem compare with the negative images of evangelism we see in our culture?
- How does the evangelism described in your poem compare to the evangelism carried out by Jesus and His disciples?
- How do you think God might be calling you to become a positive image of evangelism in someone's life?

project revolution

While in their small groups, have the students decide on a project they will complete before the next lesson. Remind them that the point of this project is to get outside the church and into the world. You will also have to choose a project yourself to model taking your faith into the world for the students.

In your small groups, write down several ideas of service or research projects that you can complete outside the church walls on your own or with your group. The suggestions in this section will help get you started.

A DIFFERENT VIEW

One great way to learn about evangelism is to talk to people who've been doing it for years. Find a fellowship group at your church that consists of some of the church's longtime members. Talk to the people in charge of this fellowship group and ask if you can bring a dessert and join the group's next gathering. Tell the group members that you simply want to hear about their positive and negative ideas of evangelism. Take note of how their views differ from your own.

BE A STUDENT

In order to care for the needs of others (as Jesus, Peter and John did) you need to figure out what those needs are. Take time this week to find out what the people close to you really need. Pay attention to how your family and friends express themselves. Ask questions and write down your findings. Do your friends need acceptance, someone to talk to or help with their homework? Do your parents need someone to pray for them, a sense of purpose in their lives or help doing the laundry? Find out this week—be a student of others!

momentum

After the students have decided on a project, have them come back together and remind them that the best way to live a life that tells the world about God's love is to read God's Word daily. They may want to follow the readings listed in this section each week and keep a journal of how God speaks to them. Be sure to remind them to check out www.SoulSurvivorEncounter.com for other ways to stay focused on God. Remember, students will follow what you do more than what you say. Make a decision to pursue God daily through His Word.

Do you feel God calling you to go deeper in your understanding of how to proclaim the good news? Explore the Time in the Word verses this week.

TIME IN THE WORD

Day 1—Romans 10:14-15
Day 2—Luke 9:1-6
Day 3—Isaiah 52:7-10
Day 4—Luke 4:16-21
Day 5—Ephesians 2:14-18

coming to a close

Throughout the New Testament, we see God using times of prayer to empower people for evangelism. You may want to vary the ways you end each meeting with prayer.

1. Turn down the lights and light two candles to help students focus. Ask them to sit silently while you read a psalm about God's call to holiness (e.g., Psalm 93). After reading the psalm, have the students pray for the person sitting on their right.
2. Have the students write out prayer requests on an index card. You can either share the requests with the whole group or establish prayer partners.
3. Ahead of time, ask one student to close the session with prayer.

AFTER THE MEETING

1. **Evaluate:** Take time to pray and ask God to give you insight into what happened during the meeting. Talk with your volunteer leaders about how God worked, what went well and what did not work. Write down your ideas for the next meeting.
2. **Encourage:** Be sure to contact each student during the week (phone calls, notes in the mail, e-mails, instant messages). As you spend time with the students outside the study, you are modeling the importance of intentionally building relationships to share God's love. Check on how they are doing in their walk with Christ this week.
3. **Equip:** Complete next week's session on your own. Keep your eyes and ears open for news stories or celebrity quotations on relationships and evangelism.
4. **Pray:** Prayerfully prepare next week's meeting and pray specifically for each student.
5. **Project Revolution:** Complete your own project so that you can talk about it next week with the students.

Note: All leader's options and tips are in shaded areas.

before everyone shows up

1. Pray for the students who attended last week. Also pray for those who did not come last week but may come this week.
2. Work through the entire session on your own during the week. As you work, think about how each student might feel about each section.
3. Think about a story you might use for the first Icebreaker option.
4. **Optional Student Assignment:** Have the students complete the study a week ahead of time.
5. Every day watch for relevant celebrity quotations and news stories that could be used to talk about relationships in the Status section. Check out www.SoulSurvivorEncounter.com for more stories and quotations.
6. Gather the material you will need for the study and be sure that all technology works.
7. View the corresponding Soul Survivor video segment ahead of time.
8. As people arrive have food and drink available to help create a welcoming atmosphere.

GETTING STARTED

1. As the students arrive, greet everyone who enters the room.
2. Pray for God's guidance as you begin the study.
3. Ask for volunteers to read the Bible passages during the study. If anyone volunteers, give him or her a sheet with the passages written on it. Be sensitive to those who may not like to read out loud.

Icebreakers

Option 1: Ask the students to briefly tell a story describing one of their really good friends. You may want to start by telling your own story. As the students tell their stories, be sure to ask them to explain how that friendship got started and what kept it strong.

Option 2: Have the students share what happened in their Project Revolution during the past week. As they share, identify how God was using relationships through their experience.

Ask the students to share any celebrity quotations or news stories they picked up during the week. Also share any that you found. Read through the quotations and interview excerpt as a group. You may want to have a copy of the entire interview on hand. Ask the students to give their impressions of the quotations and interview.

Tip: Remind the students to check out www.Soul SurvivorEncounter.com for more quotations and interviews.

WHAT PEOPLE ARE SAYING

SANDRA BULLOCK, ACTOR

"The key to any good relationship, on-screen and off, is communication, respect, and I guess you have to like the way the other person smells."[1]

MARTIN LUTHER, THEOLOGIAN

"We must reflect on God's ordered power, that is, on the incarnate Son, in whom are hidden all the treasures of the Godhead. Let us go to the child lying in the lap of His mother Mary or to the sacrificial victim suspended on the cross; there we shall really behold God, and there we shall look into His very heart. We shall see that He is compassionate and does not desire the death of the sinner but that the sinner should 'turn from his way and live.' "[2]

ANGELINA JOLIE, ACTOR

In talking about her relief work in Cambodia, Jolie said, "The most important thing, or the thing I think I accomplished most, was going to these places and sitting down with the families for about an hour, and I think . . . what matters most of all is that you go out of your way to sit down with people and listen to their stories and talk with them and show them somebody cares and is listening."[3]

JOAN BAEZ, SINGER

"The easiest kind of relationship is with ten thousand people, the hardest is with one."[4]

INTERVIEW

Subject: Martyn Layzell, Soul Survivor worship leader

Soul Survivor: How does God show up in your life? How do you see Him each day?

Martyn Layzell: I guess I feel like I meet God first and foremost through my relationships with my family. I believe that God has given the gift of marriage and family for a divine reason—so we might understand His ways more intimately. My two boys are a constant reminder of God's abundance and creativity; dealing with everyday circumstances teaches me about His grace, love and forgiveness.

See the rest of this interview and more thought-provoking quotes at www.SoulSurvivorEncounter.com.

As you come to the end of this section, encourage the students to keep their eyes and ears open for news stories and quotations for next week's topic: The Power of Story.

Show the corresponding Soul Survivor video clip from the *Living the Life & Survivors DVD*. **Option 1:** Before watching the clip, hand out pens and paper. Have the students write down their thoughts and feelings as they watch.

Option 2: Show a series of clips from *The Last Samurai* (Warner Brothers Pictures, 2003) that demonstrate how Nathan Algren builds a relationship with the samurai by becoming like them. This movie offers a secular approach to learning about another culture, which may serve as a bridge to discussing how Jesus infiltrated culture in His day.

the story

As you work through this section, think about which parts would be helpful to read as a group and which parts would be better summarized. Ask the Holy Spirit to give you guidance. You may want to take one minute at the beginning of each new section to sit quietly as each student asks God to speak to them.

THE MYTH OF ANT MAN

When Bruce Olsen was 19-years-old, he sensed God's call to share Jesus Christ with a tribe of South

American Indians called the Motilones. The Motilones were headhunters known to kill strangers.

After the Motilones beat and tortured him because he was a stranger, Olsen slowly began to build a friendship with them. As the years continued, he eventually took on their dress, their eating habits and in many ways became one of them. One day he heard a Motilone myth about anthills that gave him the avenue he needed to share the gospel of Jesus Christ. The myth went something like this:

A man had been sitting on the trail after a hunt and noticed some ants trying to build a home. He wanted to help them make a good home, like the Motilone home, so he began digging in the dirt. But because he was so big and so unknown, the ants had been afraid and had run away. Then, quite miraculously, he had become an ant. He thought like an ant, looked like an ant, and spoke the language of an ant. He lived with the ants and they came to trust him. He told them one day that he was not really an ant, but a Motilone, and that he had once tried to help them improve their home, but had scared them. The ants said their equivalent, of, "No kidding? That was you?" And they laughed at him, because he didn't look like the huge and fearful thing that had moved the dirt before. But at that moment he was turned back into a Motilone, and began to move the dirt into the shape of a Motilone home. This time the ants recognized him and let him do his work, because they knew he wouldn't harm them. That was why, according to the story, the ants had hills that looked like Motilone homes.[5]

The word "incarnation" has its root in the Latin word *carnis*, which means "flesh."[6] When people talk about Jesus as the Incarnation, they are simply saying that He took on flesh and bones. Jesus became like you and me so that we could understand how much God loves us. In the story, Olsen became like the Motilones. We're called to do the same by entering the world of those we love.

Action

Read John 1:1-5,14. How does the myth of the Ant Man help you understand why Jesus became human?

If Jesus became like one of us in order to share God's love, how does that affect how we build relationships with others?

If you watched the clips from *The Last Samurai*, have the group compare Jesus' reason for becoming like us with Nathan Algren's reasons. If you have time, have a student read 1 Corinthians 9:19-23 as a way to summarize an incarnational approach to relationships and to prepare for the next section.

ATTITUDE IS EVERYTHING

Start this section by having the students give their reasons for their answer to the question that opens this section.

Which is worse, having no friends or having someone pretend to be your friend and then finding out later that he or she was using you? In the case of evangelism, there's a fine line between genuine caring and caring for someone in order that he or she might believe.

A lot of damage is done when Christians act like someone's friend but then move on when their "friend" does not make a decision for Christ. While the Bible does talk about shaking the dust off your feet (see Matthew 10:11-15), we need to approach sharing our faith with prayer and discernment. Many people feel judged and abandoned by Christians simply because they have been judged and abandoned by Christians.

What is the difference between an authentic relationship for the sake of the gospel and a relationship for the purpose of getting a person to believe in Jesus? Attitude. In the book of Philippians, Paul wrote,

Your attitude should be the same as that of Christ Jesus (2:5).

In the original writing, the word Paul used for "attitude" is *phroneo*, the meaning of which is not simply putting on an attitude for a moment but rather having a mind-set that shapes the way you look at life.[7] We are called to look at life the way Jesus looked at life.

Action

Read Philippians 2:3-11. Then draw two columns in the space provided; label the first column "Self-Centered Evangelism" and the second column "Humble Evangelism." In each column, list characteristics of that kind of evangelism.

After the students complete this activity, discuss the students' answers. Ask God to give the students a vision for what evangelism based on authentic relationships looks like. As you come to a close, ask, "What happens when Christians don't build relationships?"

≋ break it down

As you begin this section, remind the students of the importance of spending time alone with God. Encourage them to go back to the sacred space they had last week and to begin this section by asking God to speak to the entire group.

In the Gospel of Luke, Jesus befriends a man named Zacchaeus (see Luke 19:1-10). Zacchaeus responds to evangelism in a way that is dramatically different from the way in which some people in our world today might respond to evangelism. What do you think made the difference?

Action

Read Luke 19:1-10. As you read, think about how Jesus approached this man. How does Zacchaeus's response change as the day continues? After reading the story, write a song describing Zacchaeus's response to evangelism. If you're not sure what to write, simply take a song that you like and change the words to fit how you think Zacchaeus might have felt.

≋ comeback

Have the students form small groups to share their Break It Down songs, after which they can work through the questions in this section.
   Note: Decide ahead of time whether keeping the same small groups as last week would be helpful for your particular group.

Now form small groups, read your songs aloud, and discuss the following questions. If you're working alone, read your lyrics to a friend or relative and then discuss the questions with him or her.

- In what relationships outside your church do you sense God calling you to share the good news?

- What fears do you have about taking a step to share the good news with people?
- How can you build an authentic relationship with those whom God is calling you to share the gospel?

≋ project revolution

Keeping the same small groups, have the students decide on a project they can complete this week to live out what it means to build genuine relationships. If you did not talk about last week's Project Revolution at the beginning of this session, you may want to ask students to share how their project went last week. After the groups decide on their project, have each group share what it plans to do and give the students time to pray for one another.

While in your small groups, write down ideas for a project you can do on your own or with your group outside the walls of your church. The suggestion in this section will get you started.

BECOMING AN ANT

What group of people do you sense God calling you to serve in love? Has God called you to serve a specific person or group of people at school or in your community? Is there a group that other churches seem to ignore? Take time to pray and ask God to give you His eyes as you walk around your campus or neighborhood this week. Specifically ask God whom He is calling you to love this week. Once you sense God's direction, take time to understand the needs of this person or group of people and then get creative and serve them as you build a relationship.

≋ momentum

The primary relationship that we need to focus on is our relationship with God. Encountering God daily in His Word keeps us focused on Him. Encourage students to take time each day to read God's Word and write in a journal. As a way to encourage them, let them know what you are doing and talk briefly about what you love about spending time with God each day.

A daily experience with God's Word will help you to develop authentic relationships with others. This week let these Scripture verses speak to your heart as you seek to go deeper with God.

TIME IN THE WORD

Day 1—1 Corinthians 9:19-23
Day 2—2 Kings 4:8-37
Day 3—Mark 5:21-43
Day 4—1 Thessalonians 2:6-12
Day 5—Psalm 133

coming to a close

This week, you may want to form prayer partners to end the session in prayer. Ask each person to pray out loud or silently for his or her partner and then to make a commitment to pray for his or her partner during the week. Encourage the students to check in with their prayer partners during the week.

AFTER THE MEETING

1. **Evaluate:** Take time to pray and talk with your volunteer leaders about how God worked, what went well and what did not work during the meeting. Write down your ideas to use for the next meeting.
2. **Encourage:** As the leader you are modeling how to build authentic and loving relationships for the students. Ask God to show you how to encourage each student. Take time this week to contact each student or have each of your leaders contact a small group of students.
3. **Equip:** Complete next week's session on your own. Keep your eyes and ears open for news stories or celebrity quotations on the topic of the power of storytelling.
4. **Pray:** Prayerfully prepare next week's meeting and pray specifically for each student.
5. **Project Revolution:** Complete your own project so that you can talk about it next week with the students.

Note: All leader's options and tips are in shaded areas.

before everyone shows up

1. Pray for the students in the group. Also remember to pray for their Project Revolution as they put their faith into action.
2. Work through the entire session on your own during the week. As you work, ask God to give you creativity and openness to the Holy Spirit.
3. **Optional Student Assignment:** Have the students complete the study a week ahead of time.
4. Watch for relevant celebrity quotations and news stories that could be used to talk about the use of story during the Status section. Check out www.SoulSurvivorEncounter.com for more stories and quotations.
5. Gather the needed supplies and make sure that all technology is working.
6. View the corresponding Soul Survivor video segment ahead of time.
7. Create a welcoming environment with music and light refreshments.

GETTING STARTED

1. When the students arrive, greet them and informally ask about their week.
2. Pray for God's guidance as you begin the study.
3. Ask for volunteers to read the Bible passages before the study. Have the passages printed out to give to volunteers. As always, be sensitive to those who may not like to read out loud.

Icebreakers

Option 1: Have each student or group of students share their experience with their Project Revolution. As the groups share, highlight how God is being glorified when they share.

Option 2: Have everyone in the group tell a story about what he or she did during the previous weekend. If some students do not want to share, do not pressure them. The point is to get the students both telling and enjoying stories.

This week, begin by asking the group if anyone heard or saw any interesting quotations or news stories about storytelling. After reading through the quotations, give students time to comment or ask questions.

WHAT PEOPLE ARE SAYING

JIM TRELEASE, AUTHOR

"Story is the vehicle we use to make sense of our lives in a world that often defies logic."[1]

JIMI HENDRIX, MUSICIAN

"Knowledge speaks, but wisdom listens."[2]

ROBERT MOSS, AUTHOR

"Australian Aborigines say that the big stories—the stories worth telling and retelling, the ones in which you may find the meaning of your life—are forever stalking the right teller, sniffing and tracking like predators hunting their prey in the bush."[3]

URSULA K. LEGUIN, AUTHOR

"There have been great societies that did not use the wheel, but there have been no societies that did not tell stories."[4]

INTERVIEW

Subject: Tim Hughes, worship leader, author
Soul Survivor: How, where or through whom do you experience God?
Tim Hughes: God has revealed Himself to me in so many ways that I know He's real. Reading the Bible has been a vital way of experiencing and learning more about God. Also throughout my life, as I've chosen to trust in God, I've seen that He's faithful. I remember one time when I was 19 I went to South Africa for a year with a friend. After a couple of weeks my friend got sick and had to return home. I was left feeling very alone and very scared. In that place I turned to God and prayed like mad. He was so faithful. What could have been a disaster ended up being one of the most special years of my life. When you experience God's continual faithfulness, you know He's real.

See the rest of this interview and more thought-provoking quotes at www.SoulSurvivorEncounter.com.

After discussing this section, encourage the students to watch for quotations and news stories for next week's session: Action Evangelism. Ask them to watch specifically for positive examples of people using service to share God's love.

video segment

Show the corresponding Soul Survivor video clip from the *Living the Life & Survivors DVD*. **Option 1:** Before showing the clip, ask the students to be prepared to talk about what part of the video made the biggest impression on them.
Option 2: Show one of the final scenes in *The Lord of the Rings: The Two Towers* (New Line Cinema, 2002), entitled "Tales That Mattered." Before showing this scene, ask the group to listen to how Sam describes a great story.

≋ the story

As you work through this section ahead of time, decide which parts you want the group to read and which parts you will summarize. As you begin this section, ask someone in the group to pray that God would open your hearts to receive His Word.

Imagine if a friend of yours calls you and says that he or she just had the best weekend of his or her entire life. You ask to hear about it but his or her mom yells for your friend to get off the phone and the conversation ends with, "I'll tell you about it at school tomorrow."

What would you think if on Monday morning your friend pulled out his or her laptop and played a PowerPoint presentation for you because he or she was busy talking to someone else? Or what if your friend read you a 10-page paper with an introduction, three main points and a conclusion? Would you still be interested in your friend's weekend? How would you want to hear about your friend's weekend?

You'd want to hear the story!

When people have exciting news to share, usually they tell a story. The same is true when it comes to sharing the exciting news about Jesus Christ.

THE RIGHT STYLE

There are a lot of ways to tell a story. Think about the different types of movies: western, science fiction, drama, comedy, mystery, thriller. Both authors and filmmakers are careful to pick the right style for the story they want to tell.

When Jesus' followers decided to put His story into writing, they used a style called the Gospel. "Gospel" basically means "good news." These writers wanted to be totally clear about whom they were writing. Mark declares at the start of his story that it is "the beginning of the gospel about Jesus Christ" (Mark 1:1). Although the Gospels are filled with drama, the writers weren't trying to entertain their readers as much as they were hoping to share the news about Jesus Christ.

Action

Read John 20:30-31. Can you think of a time in your life when you were certain God was working? Take a moment to tell that story to someone you know. If you are working alone, write the story down and then share it with someone later. Once you've shared your story, ask the person with whom you shared how the story was good news in his or her life.

THE MASTER STORYTELLER

Jesus liked to teach by using stories. Many times when He was asked a question, Jesus responded with a story or a parable. His parables taught us about God, and they often had a surprise ending that turned people's perceptions upside down.

In the parable of the good Samaritan, the injured man isn't helped by the religious leaders, but by the person whom everyone thought was an enemy. In the parable of the prodigal son, the young man who spends his inheritance on drinking and prostitutes is welcomed home with open arms and a party!

Jesus knew that stories are powerful and could help His listeners see God's grace in a new way.

break it down

As you begin your individual time with God, take time to pray for the others in your group and ask God to allow you to hear Him.

So far, we've been talking a lot about telling stories and parables. But a critical part of using stories in evangelism is listening to the stories of others. Nobody likes to be preached at incessantly. The importance of hearing another's story can't be overrated—when we listen to someone, we show him or her that we care. When we don't listen, we show that person that we don't really care. Read these lyrics from the song "Stories I Tell" by Toad the Wet Sprocket:

> Don't give me answers for I would refuse
> "yes" is a word for which I have no use.
> And I wasn't looking for heaven and hell,
> just someone to listen to stories I tell.
> Do we ever wonder?
> And do you ever care?[5]

Sometimes simply listening to someone's story can be an act of love that opens the door for him or her to hear the good news. Jesus not only told a good story, but He was also a good listener. He knew how to have a good conversation. One day, because He asked questions and listened well, a woman who was probably used to being ignored found a love that she never knew before.

Action

Read John 4. Evaluate Jesus' interaction with this woman and notice what He says and how He says it. Jesus breaks down the cultural norms and listens to someone on the fringe of society. Take time to pray, and then complete the following sentences in the space provided:

The people who really listen to me are . . .
The people at my work or school who are most often ignored are . . .
I sense God calling me to listen more to . . .

comeback

Have the students form small groups to share their Break It Down answers, after which they can work through the questions in this section.

Now form small groups and talk about what you wrote in response to the Break It Down activity. Listen carefully to the others in your group and answer the following questions together:

- How can you discover the stories of people whom you know?
- How can discovering their stories create a situation in which you can share how God's love has entered your life?
- What kind of story would it take to convince you to believe that Jesus died for your sins so that you might have everlasting life?

project revolution

Keeping the same small groups, have the students decide on a project they can complete this week that has to do with story evangelism. If you did not talk about last week's Project Revolution at the beginning of this session, you may want to ask the students to tell a story about how they saw God working through the project. After the groups have decided on their projects for this week, have each group describe what it plans to do.

Take some time to think of ways in which you might use stories to share your faith with your school or your community. The suggestions in this section will help get you started.

INDEPENDENT FILMMAKING

Create your own parable and make it into a movie. Use your family's camcorder or borrow a camera from a friend. Recruit friends from your church to be actors, extras, assistants, camera operators, costumers,

etc. Make sure you help others in your group make their videos—or team up and shoot a video as a group. You may also want to edit your video on one of the many video-editing systems now available. After your short film is complete, host a film festival and encourage everyone to bring friends and family. Discuss each short film made by your group, and ask others what they thought the story said about God. Then allow the screenwriter to explain his or her film's message about Jesus Christ.

GOD STORY

Write down the story of your journey with God. How did you come to know God? Was it a gradual journey, or was there a single event in which God changed your life? When have you felt close to God? When have you felt far from God? Who has affected your journey of faith? When you finish writing your God Story, share it with your youth group or church, or ask to put it in the church newsletter.

momentum

Encourage the students to read the parables of Jesus this week. You may even ask them to send you their thoughts by e-mail so that they can express how they sensed God speaking to them through each parable. This will give the students the opportunity to ask questions and help you engage God's Word together.

Take a few minutes this week to read several of Jesus' parables. What do these parables say about God's character and grace? How can these stories help you share the good news about Jesus Christ?

TIME IN THE WORD

Day 1—Matthew 18:10-14
Day 2—Luke 10:25-37
Day 3—Luke 12:13-21
Day 4—Luke 18:1-8
Day 5—Luke 16:1-15,19-31

coming to a close

Decide ahead of time how you would like to end the session in prayer. This week, you may want to consider having each small group take time to pray for the stories they sensed God wanted them to discover.

After each group has prayed together, ask God to open up the ears of each person and then close the session with silence. Encourage the students to check in with their group during the week.

AFTER THE MEETING

1. **Evaluate:** Take time to pray and talk with your volunteer leaders about how God worked, what went well and what did not go well. Write down your ideas to use for the next meeting.

2. **Encourage:** During the week take time to call, e-mail or meet with each person in the group to listen to how God is working in his or her life. Be sure to ask questions. One good way to remember your conversations is to take notes about each person after you meet with him or her, so you can refer back to your notes with specific questions next time you see that person. Ask God to show you how to specifically encourage each student. If you have a large group, assign your volunteer leaders a small group of students to call or e-mail.

3. **Equip:** Complete next week's session on your own. Keep your eyes and ears open for news stories or celebrity quotations having to do with action evangelism.

4. **Pray:** Prayerfully prepare next week's meeting and pray specifically for each student.

5. **Project Revolution:** Complete your own project so that you can talk about it next week with the students.

Note: All leader's options and tips are in shaded areas.

before everyone shows up

1. Pray for the students who attended last week. Ask God to speak to them about putting their faith into action. Pray that they have a chance to share their stories this week.
2. Check-in with each student at least once during the week to encourage him or her.
3. Work through the entire session on your own during the week. As you work, begin to envision how God may want to use this group in a significant way to influence your community. Ask God to give you creativity and openness to the Holy Spirit as you prepare.
4. **Optional Student Assignment:** Have the students complete the study a week ahead of time.
5. Watch for relevant celebrity quotations and news stories that could be used during the Status section to talk about action evangelism. Check out www.SoulSurvivorEncounter.com for more stories and quotations.
6. Gather the needed supplies and make sure that all technology is working.
7. View the corresponding Soul Survivor video segment ahead of time.
8. Create a welcoming environment with music and light refreshments.

GETTING STARTED

1. As the students arrive, have a volunteer greet everyone who enters the room.
2. Pray for God's guidance as you begin the study.
3. You might want to ask volunteers to read a selection of Bible passages to open the study. Have the passages printed out for the volunteers and remain sensitive to those who may not like to read out loud.

Icebreakers

Option 1: Have each student or group of students share their Project Revolution experience from last week. After each group has shared, explain to the students that they have already been practicing this week's topic, action evangelism.

Option 2: Have each student answer this question: How did you sense God working over the past week? You may want to start the sharing in order to give the students time to think.

WHAT PEOPLE ARE SAYING

FRANCIS BEAUMONT, PLAYWRIGHT, POET

"Faith without works is like a bird without wings; though she may hop with her companions on earth, yet she will never fly with them to heaven."[1]

ABRAHAM LINCOLN, FORMER UNITED STATES PRESIDENT

"Kindness is the only service that will stand the storm of life and not wash out. It will wear well and will be remembered long after the prism of politeness or the complexion of courtesy has faded away."[2]

BONO, LEAD SINGER, U2

In reference to the Christian response to the AIDS crisis in Africa, Bono said, "I think our whole idea of who we are is at stake. I think Judeo-Christian culture is at stake. . . . If the church doesn't respond to this, the church will be made irrelevant. It will look like the way you heard stories about people watching Jews being put on the trains. We will be that generation that watched our African brothers and sisters being put on trains."[3]

SAINT FRANCIS OF ASSISI

"It is not fitting, when one is in God's service, to have a gloomy face or a chilling look."[4]

INTERVIEW

Subject: Carla Deal, missionary
Soul Survivor: Over the past five years, what have you learned about using words and actions to communicate God's love?
Carla Deal: If there are words and no actions, then it's empty. It's all about what is already on your heart. You talk about what you are interested in. You do what you are interested in. If you do not have both words and actions, things just don't make sense. If there is a Christian who is big on service but not words, then you don't know what is really important to [him or her]. If [he or she is] big on words but not actions that just seems empty.

See the rest of this interview and more thought-provoking quotes at www.SoulSurvivorEncounter.com.

video segment

the story

Imagine going to lunch with your youth pastor after an incredible worship service. You notice a homeless woman sitting in front of the restaurant. She tells your youth pastor that she is hungry and asks for help. The pastor responds, "We can't help you with food right now, but God bless you in the name of Jesus." Then you both walk into the restaurant.
   Listen to this verse in James:

What good is it, my brothers, if a man claims to have faith but has no deeds? Can such faith save him? Suppose a brother or sister is without clothes and daily food. If one of you says to him, "Go, I wish you well; keep warm and well fed," but does nothing about his physical needs, what good is it? In the same way, faith by itself, if it is not accompanied by action, is dead (2:14-17).

That seems a little extreme, doesn't it? Maybe faith without action is coldhearted, but dead? Does God's Word really say that if we don't act on our faith, our faith doesn't exist? A major theme in the book of James is *Christianity in action*. In fact, over half the verses in James are imperatives or commands.

Allow the students to think about this before moving on.

Some would say that actions speak louder than words. The book of James basically says, "Know the Word and do it."

Action

Read James 1:22-27 and answer the following questions: What's wrong with knowing God's Word but not acting on it? Why does James talk about taking care of widows and orphans? If Christians cared for orphans and widows, what impression would the world have of the Body of Christ?

One way to get the whole group involved in these questions would be to divide students into groups of two or three students each and have the groups brainstorm as many answers as possible. After a few minutes, bring all the students together and then have each small group report to the entire group.

ARE CHRISTIANS A BUNCH OF HYPOCRITES?

Take a moment to think about one or two Christians whom you know. Now imagine they were accused in a court of law of practicing Christianity. Would there be enough evidence in their lives, outside of going to church, to demonstrate that they followed Jesus Christ?

Give the students an opportunity to answer these questions out loud. Ask them to give examples of the evidence that would be necessary to convict someone.

What about you? Does your life outside of church look any different from your friends', coworkers' or neighbors' lives? What do your everyday actions say about what you believe?

Jesus liked to preach, but He also served the needs of others. Throughout the Gospels, His words are backed up by action. In one sermon He instructed His disciples to be the same way. Check out what He said:

> You are the salt of the earth. But if the salt loses its saltiness, how can it be made salty again? It is no longer good for anything, except to be thrown out and trampled by men. You are the light of the world. A city on a hill cannot be hidden. Neither do people light a lamp and put it under a bowl. Instead they put it on its stand, and it gives light to everyone in the house. In the same way, let your light shine before men, that they may see your good deeds and praise your Father in heaven (Matthew 5:13-16).

Salt and light—both are distinctive. How can we be distinctive in a world that is so self-focused?

The answer is to act in a way that demonstrates God's love to those around us. When others ask us why we do the things we do, we can talk to them about God and direct people to Him. Listen again to Jesus' words:

> In the same way, let your light shine before men, that they may see your good deeds and praise your Father in heaven.

Action

Now read Philippians 2:15-16. As you read, think about how God may be calling you to put your faith into action in your life.

break it down

As the students prepare to spend time alone with God in their sacred spaces, ask the Holy Spirit to speak specifically to each student. Also encourage each group member to pray for the others before he or she begins.

Complete this section individually. Read the following report from Kate Lattimer, who saw lives transformed when she put her faith into action at an event called Soul Survivor The Message 2000.

Annoyed to find I was part of a Ground Level team, I didn't want to get my hands dirty and thought that I'd have no chance to evangelize. How wrong could I have been? We set to work in the garden of a tough looking 19-year-old who had just moved away from home. He was very suspicious at first, and watched us cheerfully renovate his tip of a garden—making a few sarcastic comments along the way. However, after a while, he started to ask us questions about the project, and even helped us with the work! Anyway, by the end of the afternoon he had decided to try out the evening event. He didn't just go once either—he went back, evening after evening. Who knows what affect practical love [has] had on him long-term?—Kate Lattimer[5]

Actions put Kate in a place to give glory to God. Actions will also give you the opportunity to show God's love to people in your family, school and workplace. First Peter 1:13 says, "Therefore, prepare your minds for action." Are you prepared?

Action

Answer the following questions in the space provided. Let God direct your thoughts and the words you write. Whom do you see every day who has no idea that you are a Christian? What practical needs do you see in your community?

Now write a letter to God telling Him what you sense He is calling you to do.

comeback

Have the students return to their small groups from last week to share their letters. Also encourage them to work through the questions in this section.

Now form small groups, read your letters aloud, and then discuss the following questions together. If you're working on this study alone, find a friend or parent with whom you can discuss the questions in this section.

- Do you think most Christians give an effective witness through their actions? Explain.

- Reread Bono's quotation at the beginning of this section; do you think the Church is becoming irrelevant because of inaction?
- When have you seen the love of Jesus given to a community through the actions of a group of Christians?

project revolution

As the students begin to talk with their small groups about a Project Revolution, you may want to suggest that the entire group complete an activity together this week. Working together on a project will allow the students to have a common experience of the Holy Spirit about which they can talk next week.

Write down ideas of how you can put your faith into action outside the walls of your church. You may use the suggestion in this section, or you may refer to ideas from previous sections.

ADOPT A BLOCK

Ask God to direct you to a group of houses near your church. As a group, take an afternoon to go to each house and let the residents know that you are available to help out around the house on a particular Saturday. On that Saturday, come back and serve those who need your help by cleaning, gardening or painting. Be open to how God may want to use these relationships in the future. Perhaps you may even want to come back once a month for three months as way to show the love of Christ through action!

momentum

How are you doing in your daily Bible reading? Remember, you will help the group see the importance of it through your own actions. If you have not already established accountability groups within the group, this would be a great week to start having the group encourage each other to be in God's Word daily.

If you would like to continue your study of putting faith into action, here are some Scripture passages to guide you.

TIME IN THE WORD

Day 1—Proverbs 22:9
Day 2—1 Thessalonians 4:11-12
Day 3—Isaiah 42:5-7
Day 4—1 Peter 1:13-15
Day 5—Luke 6:17-26

coming to a close

This week, begin the closing prayer by lighting a candle and turning off all the lights. Read Matthew 5:13-16 and then sit quietly. Read the passage a second time and invite the students to pray aloud if they feel like it. When the group has finished praying, read James 2:14-17 and then dismiss the students. If this feels too dramatic for your group, simply try the same prayer with the lights on and without a candle.

AFTER THE MEETING

1. **Evaluate:** Take time to pray with your volunteers and talk about how God worked, what went well and what did not go well. Write down your ideas for the next meeting.
2. **Encourage:** As a leader you are modeling how to put faith into action for the students. This week, take time to write an e-mail or a letter of encouragement to each student. Again, if your group is large, have each volunteer leader write to a small group of students.
3. **Equip:** Complete next week's session on your own. Keep your eyes and ears open for news stories or celebrity quotations on the Holy Spirit.
4. **Pray:** Prayerfully prepare next week's meeting and pray specifically for each student.
5. **Project Revolution:** Complete your own project so that you can talk about it next week with the students.

Note: All leader's options and tips are in shaded areas.

before everyone shows up

1. Pray for each student in the group this week.
2. Work through the entire session on your own during the week. As you work, begin to envision how God may use this group in a significant way to influence your community. Ask God to give you creativity and sensitivity to the Holy Spirit as you prepare.
3. **Optional Student Assignment:** Have the students complete the study a week ahead of time.
4. Watch for relevant celebrity quotations and news stories that could be used in the Status section to talk about the Holy Spirit. Check out www.Soul SurvivorEncounter.com for more stories and quotations.
5. Gather the needed supplies and make sure that all technology is working.
6. View the corresponding Soul Survivor video segment ahead of time.
7. Create a welcoming environment with music and light refreshments.

GETTING STARTED

1. As the students arrive, either you or a volunteer should greet everyone who enters the room.
2. Pray for God's guidance as you begin the study.
3. Invite students to read the Bible passages during the study. Be prepared with photocopies of the passages, but remain sensitive to those who are uncomfortable reading aloud.

Icebreakers

Option 1: Have each student share about his or her Project Revolution experience from last week.

Option 2: Divide students into groups of two students each and have each person find out three new things about the other person that they didn't already know. Then have each student introduce his or her partner to the group. By now, your students should be feeling comfortable with each other.

This week, begin by asking if anyone found interesting quotations or news stories about the Holy Spirit or evangelism. After reading through the quotations, ask the students to think about what comment or question they would have for the person who is speaking.

WHAT PEOPLE ARE SAYING

JOSH CARTER, SINGER

"I started to get a sense of conviction like I was supposed to change my direction musically. And I prayed about it a lot. And you sorta wait for, um, to see where you're led. It's hard to describe, but you feel what's right and you pray more."[1]

EVANDER HOLYFIELD, BOXER

"I was led by the spirit of God, and like I told everybody, whatever the spirit leads me to do, that's what I will do. And it wasn't nothin' so much that I did. Everybody thought that I was washed up but with God, I'm not washed up."[2]

REZA F. SAFA, AUTHOR

"As far as I am concerned, only one person can convict man of his sin, whether Muslim, Hindu, Jew, or atheist. This is the person of the Holy Spirit."[3]

DENNIS RODMAN, FORMER PROFESSIONAL BASKETBALL PLAYER

Interviewer: "Do you believe in God?"
Dennis Rodman: "I believe in the Holy Spirit."
Interviewer: "Is that a man or a woman?"
Dennis Rodman: "I try not to get the sex involved [laughs]. I think of it more like a wand waving over my head."[4]

JYRO XHAN, LEAD SINGER, FOLD ZANDURA

"In the club setting, when someone comes up to you after the show and says, 'There is something different about your music,' you know it is the Holy Spirit. I think we're always open to what God decides to do, and people's lives have been changed by the Holy Spirit at our shows. We're not trying to hide anything; there is no hidden agenda. I think the Lord uses us in spite of ourselves."[5]

INTERVIEW

Subject: Eric M. Owyoung, lead singer and guitarist for Something Like Silas
Sparrow Records released Something Like Silas's first album, *Divine Invitation*, in June 2004.
Soul Survivor: How do you know God is real in your life?
Eric M. Owyoung: I have to ask myself that in one way or another every day. Yet I come to some sort of resolution to it daily. I could tell you all these historical, biological, scientific facts about the probability of His existence, but it would mean very little to me without the personal experience of knowing Him. Everything I've ever seen in my life points to God, this whole "beautiful mess" we're in. I've seen Him in the faces of the poor in Africa, and I've seen Him in the songs of my favorite bands. I've seen Him in the silence of my quiet room before I sleep. It's just glimpses of the "reality" we call God. It's those glimpses that I live for. And somehow, He meets me in them. Someday I will see the whole face of Jesus.

See the rest of this interview and more thought-provoking quotes at www.SoulSurvivorEncounter.com.

After discussing this section, encourage the students to watch for quotations and news stories about next week's topic, Mission: Possible, a fresh look at evangelism. Specifically, ask the students to watch for positive examples of evangelism in the media.

video segment

Show the corresponding Soul Survivor video segment from the *Living the Life & Survivors DVD*. **Option 1:** Before showing the clip, ask the students to be prepared to talk about what part of the video made the biggest impression on them.

   Option 2: Show the final scene from the original *Star Wars* (Twentieth Century Fox, 1977). Show the scene where Luke receives guidance from the ghost of Obi-Wan Kenobi. After you show the scene, ask, "What's the difference between the Force in *Star Wars* and the Holy Spirit?"

As you work through this section, decide ahead of time which parts you plan to read together as a group and which parts you will summarize. You may want to begin this section by simply telling the story below instead of reading it.

Imagine that you had to go door-to-door to sell 500 candy bars. You couldn't stop until the box was empty and every candy bar had been sold. When you stop at the first house nobody is home. The people at the next house are on a diet and don't want candy. The people at the third house already bought candy bars from their nephew. There is a No Soliciting sign on the door of the fourth house. What seemed like an easy job could become discouraging very quickly.

Now imagine that you have a boss who travels the route ahead of you. This person contacts everyone along the way, finding out who likes candy and who doesn't. Even better, this person helps the people on your route work up an appetite. Best of all, your boss leads you to people who are ready to buy. All you have to do is deliver the candy.

When it comes to evangelism, the Holy Spirit is like the boss in this story. He goes ahead of us and stirs the hearts of people we meet. The Holy Spirit leads us to people who want to hear about God. Instead of having to sell Jesus to customers, our job is simply to deliver the message.

Ask the students if this description fits their understanding of the Holy Spirit. Have the students choose words that they would use to describe the Holy Spirit.

HOLY SPIRIT WHO?

The Holy Spirit is simply another way of thinking about God. Think about your dad for a minute. He's a father, he's a son, and he's also a taxpayer. Your dad has three very different roles, yet he's still the same person. In much the same way God is the Father, the Son (Jesus) and the Holy Spirit.

Many times in the Bible we see the Holy Spirit showing God's creative power. Sometimes it's said that the Holy Spirit has the special task of bringing life to something that's dead. At the beginning of the Bible, God's Spirit brings order out of cosmic chaos (see Genesis 1:2). In the New Testament, Jesus gave the Holy Spirit to His followers (see John 20:21-22).

The Bible teaches us that sin makes it harder for people to understand God or to know God (see 1 Corinthians 1:18). That's why the Holy Spirit is so important to evangelism. Before a person can understand God, he or she must be brought to life spiritually—that is where the Holy Spirit comes in.

Action

Read John 3:1-7 and 1 Corinthians 2:9-11. Describe the role of the Holy Spirit as described in these passages. Can a person know God without the Holy Spirit? Explain.

At this point you may want to tell a story of someone's trying to convince a non-Christian of God's truth in a situation in which the non-Christian totally does not get it. Then talk about how you've seen the Holy Spirit help people to understand God's truth.

MAKING THE CASE FOR EVANGELISM

The Gospel of John uses the Greek word *parakletos* to describe the Holy Spirit (see John 14:16-17) and sometimes this word is translated "comforter."[6] The Holy Spirit brought comfort to Jesus' followers after Jesus went to heaven. But part of the Holy Spirit's job is to reveal sin. He shows us how much our sins hurt others and God. The guilty feeling that we get when we become aware of our sins is sometimes called conviction.

So what is our part if the Holy Spirit convicts and comforts? Our job is simply to state what God has done in our lives. God doesn't really expect us to argue with people (see 1 Peter 3:13-17). Sometimes the Holy Spirit will make us think about someone who needs our prayers or will lead us to someone who needs to hear our story. We need to try and pay attention to the direction the Holy Spirit could be giving us.

Action

Read John 16:7-15 and Acts 8:26-39. As you read the passages, write down all the ways the Holy Spirit works in people's lives. Which actions of the Holy Spirit do you think people experience most often? Why?

A great way to end this section would be for you, or someone in the group, to talk about an experience you had in which you felt the Holy Spirit prompt you to talk to or help somebody and how you sensed the Holy Spirit moving during that encounter.

≋ break it down

If possible, have the students take their time alone with God outside. Remind them of Jesus' words in John 16:3: "But when he, the Spirit of truth, comes, he will guide you into all truth."

Take time to find a sacred space where you can work on the Break It Down section individually. Also ask God to speak to the others in your group. Then, before you complete the action step, ponder this thought: Some have described experiences where the Holy Spirit seemed to reveal Himself as a gentle breeze blowing through the trees. How does the Holy Spirit reveal himself to you?

Action

Take a moment to pray for God's Holy Spirit to come into your life. In the space provided, describe the place where you are sitting. What do you see, hear, smell and feel? How might the Holy Spirit be speaking to you? Write your own story about how you've experienced the Holy Spirit giving you direction to tell others about God.

≋ comeback

Have the students form small groups to share their stories and to work through the questions in this section.

Form groups, share your stories, and then answer the following questions:

- How did you sense the Holy Spirit speaking to you when you were alone?
- How does your experience compare with what Dennis Rodman said about the Holy Spirit in the Status section?
- Now you know the role of the Holy Spirit in evangelism—does this make sharing your faith seem easier or harder? Why?

≋ project revolution

Before the groups begin to brainstorm ideas for their Project Revolution activities for this week, remind them to pray and see if God is calling them to care for someone they served during a previous project.

Write down your ideas of how to experience the Holy Spirit outside the walls of your church. You may want to refer back to some of the ideas you've already seen in this study. Pick one project idea and go for it!

POWERED BY PRAYER

One key to becoming a better evangelist is to become a better *pray-er*. Set aside time every day this week to pray for the people at church, school and the other places you go. Ask the Holy Spirit to bring to mind people who might be ready to learn about God. If someone comes to mind, make a note to pray for him or her regularly. During your prayer time, God might give you a strong feeling that you should talk to one person in particular. It might be that God wants you to invite this person to church or a youth event or just to hang out. Follow up on this feeling. If it makes you feel more comfortable, ask a friend to go with you when you talk with this person.

≋ momentum

Encourage each student to spend time daily in Bible study. Remember, the best way for you to encourage the group to spend time in God's Word is by your example.

Don't forget to spend time reading God's Word this week. Here are five passages to help you keep moving forward with your understanding of the Holy Spirit.

TIME IN THE WORD

Day 1—Joel 2:28-29
Day 2—Titus 3:3-8
Day 3—Galatians 5:16-26
Day 4—Acts 8:26-39
Day 5—1 John 5:6-12

coming to a close

Review how your group has taken time at the end of the previous studies to close in prayer. This week, give them options of how they might want to close. You may want to suggest that this week everybody pray for everyone else in the group at the same time.

AFTER THE MEETING

1. **Evaluate:** Take time to pray and talk with your volunteer leaders about how God worked, what went well and what did not go well. Write down your ideas for the next meeting.

2. **Encourage:** Continue to contact each student during the week either yourself or through your volunteer leaders. This week, you may want to send each student a short verse as a way to encourage him or her to listen to God's voice throughout the week.

3. **Equip:** Complete next week's session on your own.

4. **Pray:** Prayerfully prepare next week's meeting and pray specifically for each student.

5. **Project Revolution:** Complete your own project so that you can talk about it next week with the students.

Note: All leader's options and tips are in shaded areas.

before everyone shows up

1. Pray for the students in the group and remember to pray as well for their Project Revolution as they put their faith into action.
2. Work through the entire session on your own during the week.
3. **Optional Student Assignment:** Have the students complete the study a week ahead of time.
4. Watch for relevant celebrity quotations and news stories that could be used during the Status secton to talk about a holistic approach to evangelism. Check out www.SoulSurvivorEncounter.com for more stories and quotations.
5. Gather the needed supplies and make sure that all technology is working.
6. View the corresponding Soul Survivor video segment ahead of time.
7. Create a welcoming environment with music and light refreshments.

GETTING STARTED

1. As the students arrive, have a volunteer leader greet each student.
2. Pray for God's guidance as you begin the study.
3. Have printed copies of the Bible passages available for student volunteers to read aloud to start the study. Be sensitive to those who may not like to read out loud.

Icebreakers

Option 1: Have volunteers share what happened during their Project Revolution this week. As they share, explain how they have already begun practicing a new form of evangelism.

Option 2: Quick thinking—Ask each student to search the room or go outside and find something that could be used as an image of evangelism. Once each student has gathered an item, give each student thirty seconds to explain why he or she chose that item.

WHAT PEOPLE ARE SAYING

JENNIFER KNAPP, MUSICIAN

"In the midst of this behavior during my freshman year, there was a girl living across the hall from me who simply loved me day after day with the love of Christ. I thought she was geeky for being a Christian, but time and time again, she'd put me to bed when I'd come home and not know which room was mine because I was so drunk."[1]

DALE THOMPSON, LEAD SINGER, BRIDE

"I did not at first accept [the] fact that God could use rock music. It took me a while to come around. By the time I accepted it as a ministry tool I was already playing it."[2]

JEFF GORDON, NASCAR DRIVER

In reference to his relationship with his wife, "That was a part of her life she did grow up with. It was important to her, and she wanted it to be important to the person she was with. A lot of the (spiritual) questions that I felt I couldn't just ask of anybody, I felt I could ask her. I really became interested in it, and my belief just grew and grew and grew. It's just continued to grow from there."[3]

MARILYN MANSON, MUSICIAN

"I was going to a nondenominational Christian school, where I was taught a very underhanded form of Christianity. For example, my Bible teacher would ask the class, 'Is there anyone in the room that's Catholic?' or 'Is there anyone that's Jewish?' If there was no response, she would talk about how wrong those other religions interpreted the Bible."[4]

INTERVIEW

Subjects: Jordan Frye and Daniel Ashby, high school students

Soul Survivor: What do you understand the word "evangelism" to mean?

Jordan Frye: I think evangelism is something very different [from] what it should be. I think it should be an overflow of who we are as Christians: our love for God should naturally flow out into the world. Seems like it's become a seminar-type thing, and we need to learn three things and we need to conduct formulas for discussion. I think that ruins the Word.

Daniel Ashby: I agree with Jordan, that it's become too robotic. Evangelism is a relationship. When you are talking with someone, it's not natural to have practiced certain phrases that you are supposed to say. Evangelism is simply talking to your friends about Christ.

See the rest of this interview and more thought-provoking quotes at www.SoulSurvivorEncounter.com.

 video segment

Show the corresponding Soul Survivor video clip from the *Living the Life & Survivors DVD*. **Option 1:** As you have done in the past, have pens and paper available for the students to write down their thoughts and feelings.

Option 2: If it is available, show scenes from the movie *Saved!* (United Artist, 2004) that demonstrate both positive and negative views of evangelism. If this movie is controversial in your church, be sure to talk about it ahead of time with your leaders and explain why you are showing it.

A few weeks ago, we started thinking about what has gotten twisted in our culture's understanding of evangelism. Now let's put a committed and authentic face on evangelism. Whether we call it missions, outreach or the authentic sharing of our faith, we don't begin with a command but with a relationship with Jesus.

Evangelism begins and ends with our love for God. Our passion to know God compels us to tell others. As our love for God grows, it is like falling in love for the first time: Our lives become focused on Jesus.

Are you passionate for God?

One of the most enthusiastic evangelists in Scripture never had any training; in fact, most people thought he was crazy, and when they tried to chain him down, he would break the chains. One day Jesus found him in the hills and cast his insanity into a bunch of pigs. After Jesus did this, He wanted others to hear this man's story. So Jesus commissioned him as an evangelist (see Mark 5:1-20).

Action

Read Mark 5:1-20. What surprises you about this story? How does the man's love for Jesus cause him to share his story? Describe a person you know whose passion for God infects the people around him or her.

Give the students some time to jot down their responses to the questions in this section before you talk as a group. You may want to follow up the descriptions of people with the discussion question, What keeps a person passionate for God?

FINAL WORDS

If you knew that you only had five minutes left to live, what would you want to say to your closest friends? Jesus' final words are recorded in Matthew 28. Historically, people have called His final words the Great Commission.

Jesus' final words to His disciples are some of His first words to us. He said, "Go and make disciples" (Matthew 28:19).

Action

Read Matthew 28:16-20. Make a list of two things: Jesus' commands and His promises. After each command and each promise, write down how each makes you feel. How does His promise make you feel?

Allow the student's time to process their feelings about Jesus' commission. Ask the students how their feelings about Jesus' words have changed over the course of this study. One way to get them to share is to ask, "What has surprised you about how you have experienced evangelism through this study?"

WAYS TO GET STARTED

What does evangelism look like? Evangelism can be a friend telling another friend how God worked in his or her life, a man helping a hungry stranger find food, a Christian becoming a dependable friend to an acquaintance at school, a person sensing God's Spirit telling him or her to do something and then doing it, a woman listening to an acquaintance and learning about her life.

The original Greek word for "evangelism" is *euaggelion*. Its most basic definition is "good news."[5] Do you want to share the good news of God's love with a world that desperately needs to hear it?

FROM YOUR LIPS TO GOD'S EARS

Remember the story of Jesus and the woman at the well (see John 4:1-42)? Jesus spent time simply asking her questions and listening to her story. In order to share the good news, He had to listen—we have to do the same.

Action

Try this simple listening exercise. Pair up with someone in your group. Ask your partner (or a friend if you're doing this study alone) to tell you a story. Be sure to ask clarifying questions as your partner talks so that you understand the story. Then repeat the story to your partner.

break it down

Remind the students that having a sacred space for quiet reflection can be something they can incorporate into their lives each day. You may also want to explain that God desires us to experience both corporate worship (i.e., a Communion service) as well as private time with Him.

As you take some individual time with God, pray for others who may be learning how to share God's love.

In his book *The Screwtape Letters*, C. S. Lewis imagined the correspondence between two demons, Screwtape and Wormwood. Screwtape instructs Wormwood in the art of keeping a man (the patient) from following God. In one letter, Screwtape writes,

Dear Wormwood, The most alarming thing in your last account of the patient is that he is making none of those confident resolutions which marked his original conversion. No more lavish promises or perpetual virtue, I gather; not even the expectation of an endowment of "grace" for life, but only a hope for the daily and hourly pittance to meet the daily and hourly temptation! This is very bad.[6]

After a study like this, you may be inspired to conquer the world for Christ. But don't let that distract you from your first love. Remember, all authentic evangelism grows out of our personal love for God.

Action

Develop a plan to spend time with God daily. Think about these things: How do you most easily hear God's voice? Who has God placed in your life who can encourage you to spend time with God? In the space provided, write an action plan to keep you focused on God daily and to help you live out what you've learned.

Now form small groups to share your plans with one another. If you're working on this study alone, find a friend to share with. Then discuss the questions in this section together.

• How will my walk with Christ be different as a result of this study?
• What can I do to help others follow through on what they sense God is calling them to do? What can others do to help me follow through on what I sense God is calling me to do?

• Do you feel God calling you to something that requires courage? Pray specifically for that situation and for the Holy Spirit to come alongside you.

Still in small groups, write down several project ideas that you can complete on your own or with your group. The suggestions in this section will get you started.

WHY REINVENT THE WHEEL?

In your group, review the Project Revolution activities you've participated in during the last five weeks. Was there one project in particular that you felt God working through? Talk about what happened. As a group, repeat one of the projects you've already done and see how God uses it this time. Then meet with your group for lunch to discuss the results. What did God do differently?

RIPPLE EFFECT

Have you noticed how throwing a rock into a pond creates ripples that slowly spread to every area of that pond? Sometimes we don't have to have a lot of Scripture memorized or an organized story to tell. But with certain people, small comments can cause ripples in their lives. This is especially helpful with people who seem resistant to hearing the gospel. But how do we do it? Make a point to casually say something about your faith to a non-Christian friend—and stop there! You are just tossing a pebble in the pond, hoping to open communication over time. For instance, if you are shopping, you might say, "Hey, we buy those donuts for our church coffee hour; they're good." Slowly, you establish that it is safe to have a conversation about church, then about God and then about Christ.

momentum

Ask the students to talk about the most helpful parts of the Momentum section so far. If they have not yet used this section, encourage them to go back over the past weeks' Scripture readings and read some of the passages as a way to continue to grow.

Do you feel God calling you to go deeper in your understanding of evangelism? Take time this week to explore the Time in the Word verses.

TIME IN THE WORD

Day 1—1 Peter 5:2-4
Day 2—Revelation 2:1-7
Day 3—Psalm 96
Day 4—James 5:19-20
Day 5—Isaiah 9:2-7

coming to a close

Read Revelation 2:2-7 as a group and ask the rhetorical question, How do you plan to remember your first love? This is not the time for answers but reflection. Ask the group to pray silently about this question. If possible, pray specifically for each person in the group. Then remind the students that this is the halfway point of the study and that next week you will study Survivors, or biblical and historical heroes of Christianity.

AFTER THE MEETING

1. **Evaluate:** Talk with the leaders about the study up until this point. You might want to experiment with a new approach for the second half of the study. Ask God to give you wisdom as you continue to lead your group.
2. **Encourage:** Continue to contact each student (through phone calls, notes of encouragement, e-mails or instant messages) and let each one know that he or she will be in your prayers. Also be sure to ask about each student's prayer requests.
3. **Pray:** Pray that you and the entire group would stay focused on God and be able to go the distance.
4. **Project Revolution:** Be sure to complete your own project.

survivors
survivors

Note: All leader's options and tips are in shaded areas.

before everyone shows up

1. Pray for the students who will attend the meeting.
2. Work through the entire session on your own and mark areas that you will focus on during the study. Ask God to give you creativity and a heart to listen to the Holy Spirit as you prepare.
3. Keep your eyes and ears open for relevant quotations or stories that demonstrate obedience. You can use these in the Status section. There are also more quotations available online at www.Soul SurvivorEncounter.com.
4. Gather materials for the study and make sure all technology works.
5. View the corresponding Soul Survivor video segment ahead of time.
6. Play music and set out light refreshments to create a welcoming atmosphere.

GETTING STARTED

1. As the students arrive, greet them, or have your volunteer leadership team greet everyone who enters the room. Begin to learn names you don't already know.
2. Pray for God's guidance as you begin the study.

Icebreakers

Option 1: Prepare slips of paper with Bible verses to be read during the meeting. When students arrive, give volunteers one passage to be read to the group. Be sensitive to those who may not like to read out loud.

Option 2: Enlist your group to make a Definition Collage at the front of the room on a white board, chalkboard or large piece of paper. Write the word "obedience" in large letters in the middle of the collage and then draw a circle around it. Ask group members to call out simple definitions of what obedience means. Write the definitions around the circle.

Read through the quotations and interview excerpt as a group. You may also want to discuss other stories or quotations you collected on that topic. Invite students to comment.

> **Tip:** The Soul Survivor Encounter website is updated periodically with new quotations, interviews and icebreakers. Check it out today at www.SoulSurvivorEncounter.com.

WHAT PEOPLE ARE SAYING

CLINT EASTWOOD, ACTOR

"There's a rebel deep in my soul. Anytime anybody tells me the trend is such and such, I go in the opposite direction."[1]

DIETRICH BONHOEFFER, THEOLOGIAN

"One act of obedience is better than one hundred sermons."[2]

DR. MATTHEW LUKWIYA, PHYSICIAN

Dr. Lukwiya was the superintendent of a hospital in Uganda during an ebola outbreak in 2000. One day a patient covered in blood fell out of bed. Nurses declined to pick the patient up, so Lukwiya did. "I will not betray my profession," he said. Lukwiya later contracted a fever and died.[3]

S. RICKLY CHRISTIAN, AUTHOR

"Your relationship with God will be marked by hardship and heartache. There will be low times when you wake up and don't feel like a Christian. There will be temptations that will sort of blitz your belief."[4]

INTERVIEW

Subject: Jon Neufeld, singer and guitarist for the band Starfield

Brothers Jon and Tim Neufeld lead Starfield, which released its self-titled first album in early 2004.

Soul Survivor: Do you have any specific role models in music and in faith?

Jon Neufeld: Our parents are very musical and brought us up singing and being involved in music. I grew up listening to the classic U2 albums *Joshua Tree* and *Rattle and Hum* but was also really influenced by artists such as Michael W. Smith, DC talk and Petra. I look up to the boldness and passion of Bono. But I also look up to worship writers [and] leaders like Martin Smith and Matt Redman. I aspire to write songs of worship and adoration the way they do. Also I love the writing of Philip Yancey.

See the rest of this interview and more thought-provoking quotes at www.SoulSurvivorEncounter.com.

video segment

Show the corresponding Soul Survivor video clip on the *Living the Life & Survivors DVD*. **Option 1:** Before the students watch the video, give each student a piece of paper and a pen or pencil. As the students watch the video, have them write down their thoughts and feelings about what is said.

Option 2: Watch a scene from the movie *The Mission* (Warner Brothers, 1986). How does the priest in this movie portray obedience amidst difficult circumstances?

≋ *the story*

As you work through this section, you may want to have the students read the different parts, or summarize each section yourself. Let the Spirit give you guidance on how to best facilitate this section. You may want to share about a time in your life when your obedience to God was challenged.

WHEN THE GOING GETS TOUGH

On the television show *Fear Factor*, contestants test their nerves by jumping off buildings, swimming under submerged girders and eating disgusting "delicacies." It takes confidence and a strong stomach to win the show. Contestants must be determined to win even when the going gets tough.

Sometimes following Christ can seem like an episode of *Fear Factor*. Difficulties can alarm us, shake us and rock our world. It takes courage and determination to be obedient to Jesus no matter the situation.

Action

In the space provided, write down something you are going through that requires confidence, courage and obedience. What feelings do you have in this situation and why?

SURVIVORS

Both history and the Bible are full of stories of people who followed Christ obediently, despite hard situations. Despite hard times and no matter what their age, these heroes believed God's promises and acted on them.

KICKED IN THE TEETH

Everyone goes through hard times—frustrations, disappointments and genuine hurt are simply a part of life. There are levels of aggravation—maybe you have a huge zit on your chin—that's a level of pain different from the level of pain you feel when someone close to you dies, but it can still mess up your day. When you experience hard times, do you ever doubt God?

Read Job 1—2:10. In this story, Job lost his family, his house, his money and his health. He was so brutally afflicted that even his wife urged him to curse God and die (see Job 2:9). Yet despite hard times, Job continued to follow God with confidence.

THE OBEDIENCE OF YOUTH

Have you ever been told you're not old enough to do something? Contrary to how you might feel, God places a huge priority on young people (see 1 Timothy 4:12). God wants you to follow Him no matter what your age.

Samuel was just a boy when God asked him to do a difficult task. God spoke to Samuel in the middle of the night. Samuel's job was to listen—to hear what God was saying and to respond to God's call. Specifically, God wanted Samuel to confront Eli, Samuel's boss, and convey a difficult message. Samuel was afraid to tell Eli, but he chose to obey God and respond to His call with confidence (see 1 Samuel 3:1-21).

Age is never an excuse for not serving the Lord—yet it's also healthy to recognize limitations of age. God will not ask us to live beyond our capabilities or the talents we've learned or been given. The point of this section is that anyone can follow Christ, regardless of age, and make a difference in the world.

OBEYING GOD

God told a teenager named Mary that she would become pregnant with the Son of God (see Luke 1:26-38). Mary's first reaction was unbelief—she wasn't sexually active (see Luke 1:34) and didn't intend to be until she married her fiancé, Joseph. How could she be pregnant?

Then an angel told Mary, "Nothing is impossible with God" (Luke 1:37). Later, Mary visited her cousin Elizabeth, who praised Mary's faithfulness by saying, "Blessed is she who has believed that what the Lord has said to her will be accomplished" (Luke 1:45). Mary obeyed the Lord throughout her pregnancy, faithfully serving Him.

At this point, you may want to have a time of prayer in which you list attributes of God and give Him glory for all He has done, weaving the experiences or specific situations of your group with praise for God's attributes.

SEEKING TRUTH

Martin Luther was a German monk who lived during the Middle Ages. Sadly, many of the Christian leaders of his day had strayed from the truth of the Bible. Church leaders sold certificates "guaranteeing" that the people who bought the certificates would go to heaven immediately upon death. The problem was that regular people couldn't discern the truth as found in the Bible from falsehood, because all the Bibles were in ancient languages. In addition to that, most people couldn't read anyway.

As a monk, Luther could read. He was struck by the simplicity of Romans 1:17: "The righteous will live by faith." Salvation doesn't happen by following arbitrary rules made up by religious leaders; Luther reasoned that it happens by faith. Luther took the risk of being harassed by religious leaders and wrote down his disagreements with the Church, which he called *The 95 Theses*. Then he nailed them to a church door—sort of the Middle Age equivalent of a TV commercial. Church leaders became angry with Luther. But soon people began to understand the truth of the Bible and stopped following the errors of the Church. Luther obediently followed his convictions and used the Bible as his guide.

You may have Catholics or former Catholics in your group who are sensitive to the Protestant overtones of Lutheranism. Try not to get bogged down in Catholic versus Protestant debates. The point is that

Luther followed God's Word, even in the face of the popular theology of his day.

≋ break it down

As before, encourage students to find their own space to work on this section individually.

Take some time to work on the Break It Down section individually.

Action

Imagine you're placed in the following situations. Write "O" in the blank provided if the situation represents obedience. Write "NO" in the blank if the situation does not represent obedience.

1. All your friends have dates for an upcoming dance. You want to go with a friend of yours, but that person tends to be a bad influence on you. You choose not to go to the dance. ____

2. An intelligent teacher speaks at an assembly at your school. She advocates an immoral position about a controversial topic. During a question-and-answer time, you go to the microphone to say something to respectfully but firmly disagree with her position. ____

3. God says He is good, but your dad just lost his job and now there isn't enough money for you to go to camp this summer. How can God be good when all this bad stuff happens? You stop going to youth group because God let you down. ____

4. You hear a spiritual friend of yours say he totally believes in something called reincarnation. Your friend says he knows this is true because he "feels" it. You search the Bible and can't find anything that agrees with reincarnation, so you decide not to believe your friend. ____

≋ comeback

Have students form small groups to discuss the questions in this section.

Take a few minutes to share your answers with your small group, and then discuss the following questions. If you're working on this study alone, find a friend or relative with whom you can discuss your thoughts.

- What does it mean to follow Christ with obedience?
- Have you ever gone through a hard time and backed away from your faith because of it? Or did you become closer to God because of it? What did you learn from the experience?
- What would you say to a friend who said, "God doesn't want me to serve Him now— I'm not old enough"?

≋ project revolution

Write down ideas for projects that you or your group will put into action this week. Read the suggestion in this section to help get you started.

TALK TO A RECOVERING ADDICT

When people become addicted to a substance or a particular behavior, usually it's because they're trying to ease some kind of pain. People can be addicted to alcohol, drugs, pornography, shopping, harmful weight-loss techniques and other things. But turning to an addiction is the opposite of obedience. Instead of turning to Christ, people often turn to something else. This week, visit with someone who is recovering from an addiction. Ask the person to tell you his or her story. How did this person get involved with the addiction? Make sure you listen and respectfully ask questions. Afterward, pray for this person and write him or her a thank-you card. Then share the results with your group.

≋ momentum

As the study comes to a close, encourage the students to continue to read Scripture and pray on their own throughout the week. Discuss what you will be doing to go deeper.

If you want to go further, check out the Time in the Word verses. Read the following passages as part of your time with God.

TIME IN THE WORD

Day 1—1 Corinthians 4:2
Day 2—Psalm 31:23
Day 3—2 Timothy 1:12
Day 4—Philippians 4:13
Day 5—2 Corinthians 12:9

coming to a close

An important part of any small group is the time spent in prayer for one another. Choose one of the following ways to close this session with prayer.

1. Have the students write out specific prayer requests on index cards. Requests can be shared with the group, or students can pair up and trade prayer requests with a partner for a week.
2. Ask one or two students to close the session with prayer.

AFTER THE MEETING

1. **Evaluate:** Close the evening by evaluating the meeting according to its purpose. Talk to your staff or student leaders about how God worked, what went well, what did not go well and what needs to be changed before the next meeting.
2. **Encourage:** Contact the students during the week via phone calls, notes, e-mails or instant messages. You may want to have the staff or volunteer leaders do this. Send cards to the new students to make them feel welcome.
3. **Equip:** Complete the next session on your own.
4. **Pray:** Pray for your students and next week's session.
5. **Project Revolution:** Complete your own project and discuss it next week with the students.

Break It Down Quiz Answers: (1) O, (2) O, (3) NO, (4) O.

Note: All leader's options and tips are in shaded areas.

before everyone shows up

1. Pray for the students who will attend the meeting and those who attended last week. As you pray, ask God to help you apply this study to your own life as well.
2. Work through the entire session on your own and mark areas that you want to focus on during the study.
3. Keep your eyes and ears open for relevant quotations or stories that demonstrate worship. You can discuss these in the Status section. There are also more Status quotations available online at www.SoulSurvivorEncounter.com.
4. Gather materials for the study and make sure all technology works.
5. View the corresponding Soul Survivor video segment ahead of time.
6. Play music and set out light refreshments to create a welcoming atmosphere.
7. Prepare a list of "dilemmas" to use if you decide to do Icebreaker Option 1.

GETTING STARTED

1. As students arrive, greet them, or have your volunteer leaders greet everyone who enters the room.
2. Have each group share its Project Revolution experience from last week.
3. Pray for God's guidance as you begin the study.

Icebreakers

Option 1: Play a game of Dilemmas. A dilemma is a choice between two undesirable alternatives. Make your list as wild as you want. Divide your students into pairs and offer a dilemma question such as "You've got to pick one of these—getting a tooth pulled or breaking a leg—which is it?" or, "You've got to jump in a swimming pool filled with moldy grapefruit or rotten tomatoes—what do you decide?" Have each student give a creative reason why he or she chose the option he or she did. Vote on the most creative answers, and then give small prizes to the winners.

Option 2: Play Two Truths and a Lie. Divide students into small groups. Have each group member tell his or her group two true statements about him- or herself and one lie. Have other group members guess which statement is the lie.

Read through the quotations and interview excerpt as a group. You may also want to discuss other stories or quotations collected this week that fit this week's topic.

WHAT PEOPLE ARE SAYING

DAVE MATTHEWS, MUSICIAN

"What in the world would I sing for if I had it all?"[1]

TOM DELONGE, SINGER, BLINK-182

"I wanted to write a song about the saddest time in my life, which is the day my parents split up, when my family just crumbled. I knew there would be a good chance that 5 percent of the kids in America would relate to it."[2]

JULIAN OF NORWICH, CHRISTIAN MYSTIC

"God, of Your goodness, give me Yourself. If I were to ask less, I should always be in want. In You alone do I have all."[3]

JIM CYMBALA, PASTOR, THE BROOKLYN TABERNACLE

"I have seen God do more in people's lives during ten minutes of real prayer than in ten of my sermons."[4]

INTERVIEW

Subject: Mike Pilavachi, pastor, author, founder of Soul Survivor

Soul Survivor: What does the word "worship" mean to you?

Mike Pilavachi: The Bible says clearly that our lives are meant to be worship before God. My most intimate times of worship with music come when that is an overflow of what is happening in my life. Biblically, worship and justice belong together. God tells us in Amos 5 that He will not listen to our music and our songs if we don't stand up for justice and the poor.

See the rest of this interview and more thought-provoking quotes at www.SoulSurvivorEncounter.com.

Show the corresponding Soul Survivor video clip on the *Living the Life & Survivors DVD*. **Option:** Before the students watch the video, give each student a piece of paper and a pen or pencil. As the students watch the video, have them write down their thoughts and feelings about what is said.

the story

As you work through this section, you may want to have the students alternate reading each section, or you may want to summarize the themes yourself. You may want to ask questions of the group as a whole or divide the students into partners to work on each section.

UNDIVIDED ATTENTION

Tom DeLazier, a North Carolina resident, can find money anywhere—but not in large quantities. DeLazier is always on the lookout for stray pennies, nickels, dimes or quarters. His vigilance paid off—in 2002 he found $2,700 in loose change.[5]

Worshiping God can be like finding cash. Anyone can find a quarter now and then—and anyone can sit in youth group and sing songs. But to truly encounter God, your worship must become part of your lifestyle.

Action

In the space provided, write down five ordinary experiences you have in the course of a day. They can be as simple as riding the bus to school, eating lunch in the cafeteria or playing video games. Beside each daily experience, write down one way in which you can make that event an act of devotion to Jesus Christ.

SURVIVORS

There are many examples of people in the Bible and throughout history who worshiped God in the good times and the bad. Their worship wasn't just about the songs; it was about who they were, what they said and what they did.

A HEART FOR GOD

As much as we grow in our faith, there are always temptations and sins to entangle us (see Hebrew 12:1). When we mess up, it's easy to get down on ourselves or want to turn away from God. But the Bible gives us an example of someone who put God first through failure as well as success.

King David messed up often in his life—especially when he sent a man to his death in order to be with the man's wife. But even through experiences of both success and failure, David always managed to return to God, repent of his sins and worship Him.

Leaders: You may want to share some examples from your life here.

THE UNNAMED WIDOW

Sometimes we think the only way to worship God is by having a large production: We need to have loud music, a huge crowd or famous preachers before God will show up. Large events can be used of the Lord, but it's important to keep perspective. Jesus says what's really important is not the scale of the worship but the attitude of one's heart in the midst of it.

In Luke 21 there is a story of a widow who gave her last two copper coins (worth less than one cent) to the Temple treasury. When Jesus saw the widow giving to the Temple alongside the rich who were depositing numerous gifts, He declared that her contribution was more valuable. He said this because she had given everything she had in the world.

WORSHIP IN THE MIDST OF PERSECUTION

Most people would say that it's pretty tough to turn the other cheek when somebody hits you across the face. People consistently frustrate, disappoint or hurt us, and our natural tendency is to hold grudges, yell or strike back. But the example of Paul and Silas offers a better way.

Action

Read Acts 16:22-34 and then write down your answers to the following questions in the space provided. What bad stuff happened to Paul and Silas? What did Paul and Silas do while in jail? Instead of letting the jailer kill himself (see Acts 16:27), how did Paul and Silas act toward him? Write one example of how someone has harmed you physically, emotionally or otherwise. Now, how can you bless that person in response?

CARING FOR THE POOR

Mother Teresa was a Yugoslavian nun who worked with lepers in India until her death in 1997. She shared the loved of Jesus and served the poorest of the poor by starting hospitals, schools, orphanages, youth centers and shelters. Her work continues today in more than 50 Indian cities and 30 countries. As part of her acceptance speech for winning the Nobel Peace Prize in 1979, Mother Teresa said, "I am grateful to receive [the Nobel Peace Prize] in the name of the hungry, the naked, the homeless, the crippled, the blind, the lepers, all those people who feel unwanted, unloved, uncared-for throughout society, people that have become a burden to society and are shunned by everybody."[6]

Action

Read the following verses and then write down answers to the following questions in the space provided. Read 1 John 3:18. What is the true way to show love for God and others? Read Matthew 10:42. This verse indicates that following Christ is not about how much we do for the Lord. If quantity of service isn't important, what is important?

The challenge here is to allow the students to think of ways they can care for others every day. They can serve God today at school, with their friends and at work. Serving God is not just something saintly nuns do.

break it down

As before, encourage the students to find their sacred space to work on this section. You may want to read Mother Teresa's prayer aloud and then play some background music while the students write out their own prayers.

Complete the following Break It Down activity individually.

Action

Read the following prayer written by Mother Teresa. Pick a phrase from the prayer that describes an incident you've gone through. In the space provided, write your own prayer.

MOTHER TERESA'S PRAYER

People are often unreasonable, illogical, and self
centered;
     …Forgive them anyway
If you are kind, people may accuse you of selfish, ulte-
rior motives;
     …Be kind anyway
If you are successful, you will win some false friends
and some true enemies;
     …Succeed anyway
If you are honest and frank, people may cheat you;
     …Be honest and frank anyway
What you spend years building, someone may destroy
overnight;
     …Build anyway
If you find serenity and happiness, they may be
jealous;
     …Be happy anyway
The good you do today, people will often forget
tomorrow;
     …Do good anyway
Give the world the best you have, and it may never be
enough;
     …Give the world the best you have anyway
You see, in the final analysis, it's between you and
God;
     …It was never between you and them anyway[7]

comeback

Have the students form small groups to discuss the
questions in this section.

Form small groups to share your prayer and then discuss the following questions. If you're working on this
study alone, find a friend or relative with whom you
can discuss your thoughts.

- How can you act graciously toward people who are unkind? How is this an act
  of worship?
- What would you say to a person who said, "I
  can't worship God at this event, they have
  the wrong kind of music"?
- How is caring for others an act of worship?

project revolution

Write down ideas for projects that you and your group
can complete outside the church walls. Read the suggestions in this section to help get you started.

The following activity could be done in one week
or over a season. Encourage anonymous giving. For
another passage on giving, check out Matthew 6:1-4.

TITHE BOX

Pick a nonprofit organization that you and your
group believe is doing good work and mark a date on
the calendar to take up a collection for that organization. You can also take up periodic collections over
a short period of time, such as a month or three
months. Decorate a box or large jar with pictures or
words that describe the organization. On the day of
the collection, have your small group or youth group
put money into the box or jar. If you only have a small
amount, give that. Give the money to the organization
you chose to support, along with a note. One youth
group of 35 students in Washington did this over one
summer and raised about $2,000. They gave half the
money to a local homeless shelter for teens. With the
other half they bought new shoes for children at an
orphanage in Haiti.

The following activity has the potential to be a truly
powerful witness. The idea is not to endorse what
you don't believe, but to care for people who need
the Lord, regardless of their beliefs or practices. As
always, caution needs to be exercised—for instance,
you probably wouldn't want your students passing
out muffins to angry protesters but allow the students to try this exercise if they're interested in pur-
suing it.

COMMON GIFTS

Choose a group of people with whom you normally
don't associate and send that group a genuine gift
that will meet its needs. Perhaps you do not believe in
the group's cause. Perhaps it's a different religious,
political or moral group. Send a note with the gift
identifying yourself and saying that you wish the
group well. For example, send a plate of cookies to
a youth group from a church of a different religion.
Send a card of encouragement to your area's political leader, even if he's unpopular.

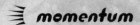 **momentum**

As the study comes to a close, encourage the students to read Scripture and pray on their own through the week. You may want to discuss what you will be doing to go deeper as well.

If you want to go further, check out the Time in the Word verses. Read the following passages this week as part of your time with God.

TIME IN THE WORD

Day 1—1 Peter 2:9
Day 2—Psalm 13
Day 3—Isaiah 40
Day 4—Nehemiah 9:5-6
Day 5—James 2:1-19

coming to a close

An important part of any small-group study is the time spent in prayer for one another. This can be done in several ways.

1. Have the students write out specific prayer requests on index cards. Requests can be shared with the group, or the students can pair up and trade requests with a partner for the week.
2. Ask one or two students to close the session with prayer.

AFTER THE MEETING

1. **Evaluate:** Discuss the evening with your staff or student leaders and evaluate how God worked, what went well, what did not go well and what needs to be changed before the next meeting.
2. **Encourage:** Contact the students during the week via phone calls, notes, e-mails or instant messages. Or have volunteer leaders do this.
3. **Equip:** Complete the next session on your own.
4. **Pray:** Pray for your students and next week's session.
5. **Project Revolution:** Complete your own project and discuss it next week with the students.

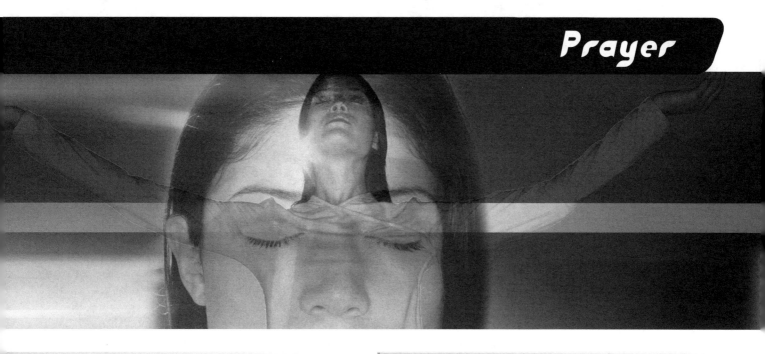

Note: All leader's options and tips are in shaded areas.

before everyone shows up

1. Pray for the students and volunteers who will attend the meeting.
2. Work through the entire session on your own and mark the areas that you want to focus on during the study.
3. Keep your eyes and ears open for relevant quotations or stories that demonstrate the power of prayer or role models of prayer. You can use these in the Status section. There are also more Status quotations available at www.Soul SurvivorEncounter.com.
4. Gather materials for the study and make sure all technology works.
5. View the corresponding Soul Survivor video segment ahead of time.
6. Play music and set out light refreshments to create a welcoming atmosphere.

GETTING STARTED

1. As students arrive, greet them, or have volunteer leaders greet everyone who enters the room.
2. Pray for God's guidance as you begin the study.

Icebreakers

Option 1: Have the students discuss their Project Revolution activity from last week.

Option 2: Sing "Happy Birthday" to everyone who has a birthday this month. Have the student come up front, introduce him- or herself and tell the group the day he or she was born and the best birthday present he or she has ever received. You may want to gather a grab bag of inexpensive gifts to hand out for birthdays.

Before you read the quotations, ask if anyone saw something in the media this week that mentioned prayer. Encourage the students to keep their eyes and ears open for spiritual quotations or themes in the media.

WHAT PEOPLE ARE SAYING

ALICIA KEYS, SINGER

"If I want to be alone, some place I can write, I can read, I can pray, I can cry, I can do whatever I want—I go to the bathroom."[1]

MARTIN LUTHER, THEOLOGIAN

"Pray as if everything depends upon God, then work as if everything depends upon you."[2]

SAINT THERESE OF LISIEUX, CATHOLIC NUN

"My life is an instant, an hour which passes by; my life is a moment which I have no power to stay. You know, O my God, that to love you here on earth—I have only today."[3]

BONO, LEAD SINGER, U2

"On New Year's Eve I always make a prayer, at midnight. If we've got rockets, we tie our prayers to them and send them off. I like the idea of beginning again. Religious folk call it being 'born again.' I think you should be born again and again and again."[4]

INTERVIEW

Subject: Rebecca St. James, songwriter, musician

Soul Survivor: Is prayer a vital part of your relationship with God or just something you do before you eat?

Rebecca St. James: Yes, it's a vital part of a relationship with God! I do pray before I eat, but to me, prayer is what empowers me to do what it is I do. I pray before I go onstage, before songwriting, before interviews. I try to pray throughout the day on decisions I'm called upon to make and to pray that my life will glorify God. I pray for certain people as people come to mind as well. Prayer is a very important part of my daily life.

See the rest of this interview and more thought-provoking quotes at www.SoulSurvivorEncounter.com.

≋ the story

As you work through this section, you may want to have the students alternate reading different parts, or summarize the themes yourself.

PRAYER IS LIKE POWER STEERING

Have you seen those gigantic earthmoving machines with tires more than six feet high? Have you ever wondered how drivers can actually steer those trucks up and down narrow dirt roads? There isn't enough muscle in 10 human arms to turn something that big, much less in 2. The secret is power steering. Sure, a driver has his hands on the steering wheel—and it looks like he's in control—but a much greater power actually turns the truck.

Prayer can be like power steering. People are the ones serving Christ in school and at work, but where does the real power come from?

Action

In the space provided, write the names of five people you know who need to hear about Jesus Christ. Beneath that, write five ways you need to grow spiritually (e.g., you need more patience). Beneath that, write five concerns having to do with your school, family, community or world that you have that seem impossible to change. Don't be afraid to dream big.

SURVIVORS

The Bible is full of people who lived out the very words of Ephesians 3:20-21: "[God] is able to do immeasurably more than all we ask or imagine." Their lives stand as examples of what can happen when people dream big with God.

THE PRAYER OF ELIJAH

Sometimes God calls us to confront sin. Maybe it's the sin in others' lives; maybe it's the sin in our own lives. Elijah was a prophet who confronted the false spiritual leaders of his day. Although people knew God's truth, they wavered back and forth worshiping idols and false gods. But Elijah took a stand for righteousness in a rip-roaring showdown for the Lord.

Action

Read 1 Kings 18:16-40 and then answer the following questions: What kind of contest did Elijah propose with the prophets of Baal? What steps did Elijah take to make the contest more difficult for himself and the Lord (see vv. 33-35)? Why do you think he did that? What was the focus of Elijah's prayer in verses 36-37? At its core, what was this contest all about?

THE PRAYER OF JEHOSHAPHAT

Jehoshaphat, a king of Judah, found himself in a seemingly impossible situation. He worried because a huge army was marching against him, but instead of panicking, he prayed to the Lord. Jehoshaphat admitted that he had no idea what to do (see 2 Chronicles 20:12), yet his eyes remained on God.

In Jehoshaphat's prayer, he reminded God of several past actions God had taken and told God that the invading army was mocking Him (see 2 Chronicles 20:6-12). Then God sent a message to one of Jehoshaphat's priests, saying that the coming battle was God's to fight. So the next day, Jehoshaphat marched his army out to meet the invading force, sending men out in front of his army to sing praises to God. Very soon his army found the invaders already ambushed and defeated on the battlefield—God had answered Jehoshaphat's prayer in a huge way!

THE PRAYER OF JOSHUA

Joshua was a military commander of Israel who needed to decide whether to fight a massive army of combined enemies. Joshua knew the battle would be strategic. If he defeated his enemies all at once, he wouldn't have to spend as much time, energy or resources waging separate campaigns against each one. Still, the numbers were stacked in his enemies' favor.

Action

Read Joshua 10:1-15 and then answer the following questions: The people of Gibeon tricked the Israelites into an alliance (see Joshua 9). What does Joshua's willingness to help them anyway say about his character? Why did God tell Joshua not to be afraid (see Joshua 10:8)? When God intervenes on our behalf, what sort of responsibilities might we have in the situation? List some examples.

When we pray, we can rest in God's sovereign provision for the outcome He desires—still, God's provision often involves our action. There's an old illustration you might use that shows this: One day a man is trapped on the roof of his house during a flood. He prays for help. A boat captain comes by and offers to row the man to shore. "No thanks," the man replies, "God is going to save me." A helicopter pilot comes by with the same offer. The man gives the same reply. Finally the waters rise and the man on the roof drowns. In heaven, he asks God why He didn't help. "I did," God says. "I sent the boat and the helicopter. Your responsibility was to accept their help!"

THE PRAYER OF ELISHA

One day a small army of foes came to kidnap Elisha because he had warned the king of Israel about a foreign ambush and attack—information Elisha had received from God. One morning, Elisha's servant awoke, went outside and found himself surrounded by enemies looking for Elisha. The servant ran to tell Elisha, who calmly said, "Don't be afraid. . . . Those who are with us are more than those who are with them" (2 Kings 6:16). But his servant was flustered, so Elisha asked God to open the servant's eyes, after which the servant saw the surrounding hills filled with horses and chariots of fire. Elisha asked God to blind the small army of enemies, and God granted his request! Then Elisha led the small kidnapping army to Samaria, but instead of having them killed, Elisha had a feast prepared for them and sent them on their way.

The story of Elisha shows how God can work powerfully through prayer, even in the worst situations.

⮚ break it down

This section encourages students to think about "impossible" situations where God has intervened for His glory.

Read the "impossible" situations listed below, and then put a check mark by "T" for true if you think the statement actually happened, or "F" for false if you think the statement did not actually happen.

1. The leader of one of the toughest street gangs in New York City, a young thug named Nicky Cruz, known for murder, violence, drugs and

involvement in the occult, became a Christian and his life completely changed. ___T___F

2. Abortion was made legal in the United States. ___T___F

3. Two college students in California began to pray for their state's governor. One weekend, they decided to drive to the state capitol to tell the governor about Jesus Christ. Along the way they shared their faith with two gas-station attendants, four security guards, the head of the United States National Guard, the director of the state Department of Education, the head of the California Highway Patrol, the governor's secretary and the governor himself. ___T___F

4. Slavery was outlawed in the United States. ___T___F

5. A hostile tribe of South American indians murdered five missionaries in the jungles of Ecuador. Later, two of the missionaries' wives returned to the tribe. Many in the tribe came to know Jesus. ___T___F

6. Pornography was outlawed in the United States. ___T___F

7. Communism, a political system dedicated to atheism (the belief that there is no God), fell apart in Russia. ___T___F

8. World hunger was eradicated forever. ___T___F

comeback

Have your students form small groups and discuss the following questions. Then encourage each group to spend a good amount of time praying together.

Form small groups and share your Break It Down answers and then discuss the following. If you're working on this study alone, find a friend or relative with whom you can discuss your thoughts.

- How is prayer like the power steering of an earthmoving machine?
- What is one thing about prayer that you've learned so far?
- Spend some time praying, alone or with your group. Pray together about pressing personal or group requests.

project revolution

Write down ideas for a project that you or your group can complete outside the church walls this week. Read the following suggestion to help you get started.

PRAYER LETTER

Write a letter to the editor of your local newspaper, encouraging prayer for an item of concern in your community or area. Keep it short, professional, sincere and positive. Use language and expressions that your newspaper's readers are familiar with. You may want to use a template like the one below.

To the editor:

Like many in this area, we are very concerned about [insert concern] and want to suggest a faith-based means as part of this problem's remedy. On [insert date and time] we encourage everyone who believes in prayer to ask for God's wisdom and help in this matter. We take literally the words of Ephesians 3:20-21: "[God] is able to do immeasurably more than all we ask or imagine."

Sincerely,

[Sign your name(s)]

momentum

As the study comes to a close, encourage the students to read Scripture and pray on their own through the week.

If you want to go further, check out the Time in the Word Scripture verses on your own this week.

TIME IN THE WORD

Day 1—1 Thessalonians 5:17
Day 2—Matthew 6:9-13
Day 3—1 Chronicles 4:9-10
Day 4—James 5:13-19
Day 5—Psalm 5

coming to a close

An important part of any small-group study is the time spent in prayer for one another. This can be done in several ways.

1. Have the students write out specific prayer requests on index cards. Requests can be shared with the group, or the students can pair up and trade requests with a partner for the week.
2. Ask one or two students to close the session with prayer.

AFTER THE MEETING

1. **Evaluate:** Discuss the evening with your volunteer leaders and evaluate how God worked, what went well, what did not go well and what needs to be changed before your next meeting.
2. **Encourage:** Contact the students during the week via phone calls, notes, e-mails or instant messages. You may want to have volunteer leaders do this.
3. **Equip:** Complete the next session on your own.
4. **Pray:** Pray for your students and next week's session.
5. **Project Revolution:** Complete your own project and during the next session share what happened with the students.

Break It Down Quiz Answers: (1) True, (2) True, (3) True, (4) True, (5) True, (6) False, (7) True, (8) False.

Forgiveness

Note: All leader's options and tips are in shaded areas.

before everyone shows up

1. Pray for the students and volunteers who will attend the meeting. As you pray, ask God to help you apply this study to your own life where necessary.
2. Work through the entire session on your own and mark the areas that you want to focus on during the study.
3. Keep your eyes and ears open for relevant quotations or stories that demonstrate forgiveness. You can use these in the Status section. There are also more Status quotations available online at www.SoulSurvivorEncounter.com.
4. Gather materials for the study and make sure all technology works.
5. View the corresponding Soul Survivor video segment ahead of time.
6. Play music and set out light refreshments to create a welcoming atmosphere.

GETTING STARTED

1. As the students arrive, have the volunteer leaders greet everyone who enters the room.
2. Pray for God's guidance as you begin the study.

Icebreakers

Option 1: Once all the students have arrived, ask them to introduce themselves to someone they don't know very well. Give the students two minutes to ask what kind of candy bar the other person would be if he or she could be any type and why. Have the students share their findings with the entire group.

Option 2: This icebreaker is called Human Bingo. Prepare a bingo-style grid of unusual facts or experiences to which people in your group will relate (e.g., has braces, owns a pair of snow skis, has a relative in the military, is left-handed). Photocopy the bingo sheets and hand them out to the students as they arrive. Have the students mingle with each other to find someone who can sign off on a square. Each student can only sign off on one square on another student's bingo sheet. The winner is the first person who fills up his or her entire grid with signatures—or the person who gets the most signatures in the time allotted for the activity.

WHAT PEOPLE ARE SAYING

CHRIS MARTIN, LEAD SINGER, COLDPLAY

When asked about the relief work of U2's Bono, Martin said, "I see Bono actually getting things achieved. While everyone else is swearing at George Bush, Bono is the one who rubs Bush's back and gets a billion dollars for Africa."[1]

J. STEPHEN ALESSI, MIAMI PASTOR

"For [Tammy Faye (Bakker)] to be able to stand up, with all the hurt, and not take a bottle of pills or blow her brains out, that gal has something inside of her a lot of people don't have."[2]

BOB BRINER, AUTHOR

"The only way we can really change the world is to immerse our wills and desires so completely in the mind of Christ that we become extensions of His ministry to mankind. The best way to do that is to pray."[3]

DEAN BATALI, SCREENWRITER, PRODUCER

"Hollywood is junior high school with rich, angry people. . . . I don't think a day goes by when I'm not chided or attacked for my Christianity."[4]

INTERVIEW

Subject: Don Williams, speaker, author
Soul Survivor: What can young people do if they've given in to sin and done something they regret?
Don Williams: We are all in this boat and traditional answers work: repent, receive forgiveness and recommit your life to Christ. In other words, the center of our faith is the Cross. God forgives us in His Son. We simply must receive His grace—fully available, Luke 15. But James 5 also works—we need to confess our sins to each other and pray for each other. Healing is found here. It also helps to see why we have fallen into this particular sin. What is the route that has taken us there? How can we protect ourselves from behaviors like this in the future? What can we learn and what is God teaching us from this? All of this helps us to find the way out.

See the rest of this interview and more thought-provoking quotes at www.SoulSurvivorEncounter.com.

≶ **the story**

As you work through this section, you may want to have the students alternate reading different parts, or summarize important themes yourself.

LIFE IS NOT FAIR

How many times have you heard that? It's true. The world can be an unjust place. Children suffer in war. Typhoons rip apart coastal communities. Friends die in car accidents. Perhaps you're going through a hurtful situation right now. Questions come up: How could God allow this? or Will this situation ever get better? or How should I feel in the midst of this hurt?

Action

In the space provided, list five concerns involving other people that you feel are unresolved or awkward. Just list them as quickly as you think of them.

SURVIVORS

God calls us to a place of radical caring and forgiveness as Christians, but we can't do it alone. We simply don't have enough power, strength, wisdom or love. But when we ask for God's compassion and forgiveness to help us forgive others, amazing things can happen. Check out the examples in this section.

JOSEPH AND INJUSTICE

Joseph was the favored son of a wealthy nomad, but his life fell apart at age 17 when his older brothers sold him into slavery (see Genesis 37—41). Then it got worse. As a slave, Joseph refused to sleep with a conniving seductress, so she had him thrown into prison. But throughout his trials, Joseph kept his eyes on God. Then, in a bizarre set of circumstances, Joseph found himself very suddenly rising from the prison to the second-in-command over all of Egypt, a superpower country at that time. In his new position, Joseph was in charge of a project that saved thousands of people from starving to death—including his own brothers who once betrayed him.

But Joseph was able to forgive his brothers completely, look on them with love and help them immensely when they needed help. Joseph's forgiveness and grace is a great example for all of us.

JONAH AND COMPASSION

God called the prophet Jonah to preach to a city known for its sinful people. Jonah's first reaction was to run in the opposite direction (see Jonah 1—4). Eventually, after running away, sailing through a storm, getting swallowed by a whale and later being spit up on a beach, Jonah did what God had asked. Then, when Jonah delivered God's message to this city full of sinful people, they repented and turned to the Lord. But Jonah wasn't happy—he wanted God to show His wrath on the sinful people for their sin, not forgive them.

How difficult is it to for us to have compassion for people who don't deserve it? Jonah's life illustrates God's radical call to compassion and forgiveness. Our challenge is to do what seems unnatural—to love when it's hard, to forgive when you don't want to, to show mercy when someone deserves nothing.

You may want to take the students directly to the text here, particularly Jonah 4. The key questions here are Why is Jonah so angry at God's decision not to bring havoc on the city? How does that relate to Jonah's sitting underneath a vine? Key verse: Jonah 4:11.

CORRIE TEN BOOM AND FORGIVENESS

Corrie ten Boom hid Jews in her home in the Netherlands during World War II. Later, Nazi soldiers arrested her and took her to a Nazi concentration camp. After the war, she wrote about meeting one of her former jailers, someone who had mocked her and watched as her sister died in the concentration camp. But her former jailer had since become a Christian:

He came up to me as the church was emptying. "How grateful I am for your message," he said. "To think that, as you said, He has washed my sins away." His hand was thrust out to shake mine. I, who had preached so often the need to forgive, kept my hand at my side. I tried to smile, I struggled to raise my hand. I could not. I felt nothing, not the slightest spark of warmth or charity. And so I breathed a silent prayer. *Jesus I cannot forgive him. Give me Your forgiveness.* As I took his hand the most incredible thing happened. From my shoulder along my arm and through my hand a current seemed to pass from me to him, while into my heart sprang a love that almost overwhelmed me. When [Christ] tells us to love our enemies, He gives, along with the command, the love itself.[5]

When you experience injustice, Christ calls you to forgive. You don't have to pretend that the evil never happened—God agrees that wrong is wrong. But the only way for you to have true peace is to forgive the other person.

Forgiveness can be a tricky issue, particularly if the students are in painful situations. Boundaries may need to be set. For a complete treatment of the subject, see R. T. Kendall's book *Total Forgiveness.*

JESUS, FORGIVENESS INCARNATE

Jesus' life on Earth was all about offering people forgiveness when they didn't deserve it. Jesus' work on the cross wasn't simply dying for us—anyone can die for another person; people do it all the time in wars. The amazing thing about the Cross is that Christ *took on hell* for us. Instead of allowing us to experience separation from God, Christ experienced it for us and took all our sins on Himself. What was that like for Jesus? He was punished for every murder, every rape and every sin while He hung on the cross that day.

Action

Read Romans 5:6, Galatians 3:13 and 1 Peter 2:24. Write in your own words what Christ's death on the cross means for people around the world as you understand it from these verses.

Now may be a good time to have a short time of worship together.

≡ break it down

Pray that the students will allow the Holy Spirit to work through this section as they work on it individually.

Complete the following Break It Down activities individually, if possible, in your personal or sacred space.

GIVE INJUSTICE TO GOD

Pray through the five items you listed in the first action step in the Story section and transfer these anxieties from your own care to God's. Ask God to help you forgive the people involved that you need to forgive.

Action

Then, with your list in hand, pray through the following prayer:

Lord, I can't deal with these things on my own—but You can. You have the wisdom, strength, power and love to handle all that concerns me. Right now I want to pray the theme of 1 Peter 5:7—and I cast all my cares on You. I also pray the theme of 2 Corinthians 12:9—and I declare that Your grace is enough, and Your power works even though I'm weak. Finally, I want to take literally the words of 1 Thessalonians 5:18—and I give You thanks in this situation and all situations. Somehow You will use these experiences on my list for Your glory. That is what I pray for today. Thanks, Amen.

Action

To help you remember this moment, write down in the space provided any thoughts you have about what you've just prayed. If other concerns come to mind, write them down and pray for them now.

comeback

Have the students form small groups and discuss the following questions. Encourage them to close the Comeback time with prayer.

Form small groups to discuss the following questions. If you're working on this study alone, find a friend or relative to discuss your thoughts with.

- What do you think when you hear Christians say, "One day it will all work out for the best"? Do you believe that?

- Do you think God calls us to compassion? Is compassion a calling or something different?
- When you are the victim of an unjust act, Jesus calls you to forgive the person responsible. But how do you know when you've forgiven someone?

project revolution

Write down ideas for projects that you can complete outside the church walls and choose one that you or your group will put into action this week. Read the suggestion in this section to help you get started.

FORGIVENESS WALK

Create a "Forgiveness Walk" in a public area—but make sure you first get permission from whomever owns the property. Set up five or six stations that represent different aspects of forgiveness. At each station, have some kind of artwork, a collage, a verse of Scripture, a prayer, a station for people to write or draw or anything else that is appropriate to allow people to reflect on and experience forgiveness. Number the stations and allow people to walk through the various stations at their own pace. You also might want to create flyers listing the location and time and invite people to experience your Forgiveness Walk.

momentum

As the study comes to a close, encourage the students to read Scripture and pray on their own through the week.

If you want to go further, check out the Time in the Word verses. Read the following passages this week as part of your time with God.

TIME IN THE WORD

Day 1—2 Corinthians 8:9
Day 2—Philippians 2:5-7
Day 3—1 John 3:16
Day 4—2 Corinthians 5:14-15
Day 5—Isaiah 53:4-12

coming to a close

An important part of any small-group study is the time spent in prayer for one another. This can be done in several ways. This week gather as a group and allow the students to pray aloud as they feel led. Designate one student to open the prayer and another to close it.

AFTER THE MEETING

1. **Evaluate:** Discuss the evening with your volunteer leaders and evaluate how God worked, what went well, what did not go well and what needs to be changed before your next meeting.
2. **Encourage:** Contact the students during the week via phone calls, notes, e-mails or instant messages. You may want to have your staff or volunteer leaders do this.
3. **Equip:** Complete the next session on your own.
4. **Pray:** Pray for the students and next week's session.
5. **Project Revolution:** Complete a project and discuss it next week with the students.

Note: All leader's options and tips are in shaded areas.

before everyone shows up

1. Pray for the students who will attend this study. Ask the Holy Spirit to guide you as a teacher and the students as they learn.
2. Work through the entire session on your own and mark the areas that you want to focus on during the study. If you have a student leadership team, consider assigning various portions of the study to student leaders to lead, but give them time to prepare.
3. Watch for relevant celebrity quotations and news stories that could be used to discuss faith. You can use these in the Status section. Check out www.SoulSurvivorEncounter.com for more stories and quotations.
4. Gather the needed supplies and make sure that all technology is working.
5. View the corresponding Soul Survivor video segment ahead of time.
6. Create a welcoming environment with music and light refreshments.

GETTING STARTED

1. As the students arrive, greet them, or have the volunteer leaders greet them.
2. Pray for God's guidance as you begin the study.

Icebreakers

Option 1: Once all the students have arrived, ask them to introduce themselves to someone they haven't met before or don't know very well. Give the students two minutes to ask another person where he or she most wants to visit and why. Have the students share their findings with the entire group.

Option 2: This activity is called the Blindfold Walk. Pair up students and give one student in each pair a blindfold. Have the "seeing" students walk the blindfolded students around the building without steering them physically, using voice commands only. Switch blindfolds and have each pair try it again. You might want to talk about how faith in God can be similarly scary.

⦚ status

Read through the quotations and interview excerpt as a group. You may also want to discuss other stories or quotations collected this week that fit this week's topic. As always, invite the students to comment.

WHAT PEOPLE ARE SAYING

WAYNE GRETZKY, FORMER HOCKEY STAR

"You miss 100 percent of the shots you never take."[1]

BRENT BRADLEY, AUTHOR

"God does not come to be enlisted in our cause, but to enlist us in His."[2]

ABRAHAM LINCOLN, FORMER UNITED STATES PRESIDENT

"Faith is not believing that God can, but that God will!"[3]

BROTHER ANDREW, MISSIONARY

"God is a God who answers prayer. Ask the biggest things of God, and expect the biggest answers through faith and prayer."[4]

INTERVIEW

Subject: Tommy Walker, worship leader, author
Worship leader Tommy Walker has written numerous worship songs including "He Knows My Name," "Mourning into Dancing" and "No Greater Love." His first book, *He Knows My Name*, was released in October 2004.

Soul Survivor: Did you have role models that you looked up to as a young person?

Tommy Walker: Yes, many of my family members are in ministry and were great role models to me. I think this is very important. Young people should seek them out, go hang out with them and constantly ask questions!

SS: Have you written any new songs lately?

TW: Yeah, I just wrote one called "All About Your Glory." It's about letting every area of my life be like a worship song to God.

See the rest of this interview and more thought-provoking quotes at www.SoulSurvivorEncounter.com.

⦚ the story

As you work through this section, you may want to have the students alternate reading different parts, or summarize the themes yourself.

A CLEAN SLATE

The Discovery Channel recently aired a show called *Humanimals*, featuring the stories of people who go to extreme lengths to resemble animals. The Lizard Man is a tame example—he's got a forked tongue. What about the guy who grafted horns to his forehead? Or Cat Man, who not only had his body tattooed with stripes from head to toe but also got latex whisker implants, had his teeth filed and his lip surgically altered into a snarl?[5]

Sometimes we fear that if we're totally dedicated to Jesus Christ, He will call us to do something similarly bizarre—such as live in the jungle or wear ugly clothes for the rest of our lives. But if God truly wants the best for us, should we really fear a life lived by faith?

Action

If your life were a blank sheet of paper, could you sign your name at the bottom, hand it over to Jesus Christ and say, "Write whatever You want, my life is Yours." In the space provided, write how you feel about living by faith and putting your life in God's hands.

As an added visual teaching device, you may want to have a large blank sheet of paper up front with a place to sign at the bottom. Allow time for the students to share what they've written about if they so choose.

SURVIVORS

People throughout history have taken massive steps to put their faith in God. Oftentimes, their lives had been radically changed, and subsequently, they helped shape the world. By looking at their lives, we can see that living by faith is nothing to dread, but in fact, something to strive for.

ABRAHAM—HOLDING NOTHING BACK

God had made a promise to Abraham that one day he would become the father of a great nation (see Genesis 12:2; 15:4-5). There was only one problem: Abraham was really old and had no kids. Finally, when Abraham's wife did have a son, they were both senior citizens—go figure. They named their son Isaac, which means "laughter" (see Genesis 21:1-7). Then God asked Abraham to take Isaac into the wilderness and sacrifice him. Suddenly, Abraham was faced with a dilemma—he knew God has planned the future around Isaac, but he also knew God wanted him to give Isaac up. Abraham could not reconcile the two ideas, but he believed God was good and so he obeyed God and took Isaac out into the wilderness.

Action

Read Genesis 22:1-18. What does it mean to give everything to God? If God is truly good, can He be fully trusted? In the space provided, write your thoughts about Abraham's situation and how it was resolved.

FOUR FRIENDS—PUTTING FAITH INTO ACTION

Living for Christ can seem like doing two opposite things at the same time—on one hand, we're called to "be still, and know that [He is] God" (Psalm 46:10). On the other hand, faith is dead if not accompanied by action (see James 2:17). So which is it? How can we be still and active at the same time?

Mark 2:1-12 tells the story of four friends who brought a fifth friend to see Christ. Their buddy was in bad shape; he was paralyzed, and his friends had to carry him on a stretcher. But the house where Jesus was preaching was overflowing with people and the four friends couldn't get their buddy inside. So they improvised. They trusted Christ so much that they climbed the walls of the house, ripped a hole in the roof and lowered their friend down through the roof. Christ forgave the sick man's sins, healed him and commended the faith of his four friends.

MOSES—LOOKING AHEAD TO REWARD

When it feels as if you're in an impossible situation, look ahead to the reward you'll have in heaven. Moses lived out that kind of faith. He never considered himself a public figure; he even had trouble with public speaking, yet God called him to lead an entire nation from slavery to freedom.

Action

Read the summary of Moses' life of faith in Hebrews 11:24-29. Pick one of the areas in which Moses showed great faith and write it below. Underneath that, write one way you can show that same faith in your life.

BROTHER ANDREW—A LIFE OF FAITH

In the 1950s, '60s and '70s, a Dutch missionary named Brother Andrew gained a reputation for smuggling Bibles into countries in which Bibles were illegal. Sometimes he would hide Bibles in his car while going through border crossings; other times he would leave Bibles in plain view on the front seat of his car as an act of faith.

In 1981, Brother Andrew helped smuggle over 1 million Bibles into communist China. From the early 1990s until today, his organization, Open Doors, has focused on Muslim countries, Eastern Europe, Latin America, Africa and Asia. He has met with Yasser Arafat and others reportedly hostile to Christians. In 1997, the World Evangelical Fellowship honored Brother Andrew as "legendary."

≩ break it down

The following exercise can be extremely powerful. The goal is to create opportunities for deep questions, soul searching and reflection. Pray that the Holy Spirit would search out the students' minds and hearts as they consider starting a Whatever Journal.

Complete this Break It Down activity individually in your sacred space. God is prepared to give you a wild and passionate life, but He wants to hear one small word. What's the word? "Whatever." Not *whatever* in the sense that you couldn't care less, but *whatever* in the sense of whatever He wants and whatever it takes. Saying "whatever" means that you're asking Him to write His story for your life.

Action

Begin a Whatever Journal. Using a pad of paper, notebook or journal, start writing down prayer requests, answered prayers, Scripture and other stories. Right now, write a prayer telling God that you're willing to do *whatever* He wants you to. Place this prayer at the start of your Whatever Journal and then continue to write in it every chance you get.

comeback

Now form small groups and discuss the following questions. If you're working on this study alone, find a friend or relative to discuss your thoughts with.

- What does it mean to live by faith?
- When you live by faith, how can you be both "still" and "active" at the same time?
- How can looking ahead to God's reward help you live by faith in your daily life?

Spend some time praying as a group. Pray that God would give the students the courage and peace necessary to live a life of faith.

project revolution

Still in your small groups, come up with a unique project that you can complete outside the walls of the church. The suggestion in this section will get you started.

CREATE A MARKER

Create a personal marker that will help you remember your decision to say "whatever" to God, as in "whatever you want me to do." You can make this project as creative and as personal as you like. Take a walk to some place that you pass often—maybe a park, neighborhood or even a city street. At a location of your choosing, leave something behind that will help you remember your decision to live by faith. Perhaps you want to leave a rock in a nearby garden. One student who did this exercise left a watch in a tree to remember he was leaving something behind that he once thought of as valuable. Be careful not to leave something that might be considered litter. Perhaps you could symbolically throw something away. When you place your item wherever you decide, pray that God would help you remember this moment every time you pass that particular spot.

momentum

As this section comes to a close, encourage the students to read Scripture and to pray on their own throughout the week. Reading the verses below is one option to go deeper. Reminder: There are many other options available at www.Soul SurvivorEncounter.com.

If you want to go further this week, check out the following Scripture verses.

TIME IN THE WORD

Day 1—Luke 17:5
Day 2—Hebrews 11
Day 3—Romans 12:2
Day 4—Psalm 46
Day 5—Habakkuk 2:4; Romans 1:17; Galatians 3:11; Hebrews 10:38-39

coming to a close

An important part of any small-group study is the time spent in prayer for one another—end the study time this week by going outside and praying for your community in front of the church or youth room. Either have several students pray for specific community concerns, or have several of your volunteer leaders pray for specific community concerns.

AFTER THE MEETING

1. **Evaluate:** Discuss the evening with your staff or volunteer leaders and evaluate how God worked, what went well, what did not go well and what needs to be changed before the next meeting.
2. **Encourage:** Contact the students during the week via phone calls, notes, e-mails or instant messages. You may want to have your volunteer leaders do this.
3. **Equip:** Complete the next session on your own.
4. **Pray:** Pray for the students and next week's session—the final session of this study.
5. **Project Revolution:** Complete a project and discuss it next week with the students.

Note: All leader's options and tips are in shaded areas.

before everyone shows up

1. Pray for the students who will attend the meeting. Ask the Holy Spirit to guide you as a teacher and the students as they learn.
2. Work through the entire session on your own and mark the areas that you want to focus on during the study.
3. Watch for relevant celebrity quotations and news stories that could be used to discuss love. You can use these in the Status section. Also check out www.SoulSurvivorEncounter.com for more stories and quotations.
4. Gather the needed supplies and make sure that all technology is working.
5. View the corresponding Soul Survivor video segment ahead of time.
6. Create a welcoming environment with music and light refreshments.
7. If you decide to do Icebreaker Option 2, set out large sheets of cardboard and a variety of magazines, glue, scissors and colored markers.

GETTING STARTED

1. As the students arrive, greet them, or have the volunteer leaders greet them.
2. Pray for God's guidance as you begin the study.
3. Ask the students if they would like to read the Bible passages during the study. If anyone volunteers, give him or her a sheet with the passages written on it. Be sensitive to those who may not like to read out loud.
4. Have the volunteers discuss their experience with last week's Project Revolution activity.

Icebreakers

Option 1: Once all the students have arrived, ask them to introduce themselves to someone they don't know very well. Give the students two minutes to ask another person what he or she wants to be when he or she grows up and why. Then ask volunteers to share their findings with the group.

Option 2: This activity is called True Love Collage. Set out large sheets of cardboard and a variety of magazines, glue, scissors and colored markers. Invite the students to cut out pictures and words or to write poems that illustrate true love.

Read through the quotations and interview excerpt as a group. You may also want to discuss other stories of quotations collected this week that fit this week's topic.

WHAT PEOPLE ARE SAYING

DR. PHIL McGRAW, TALK-SHOW THERAPIST

"The true friend is the one that's coming in the door while everyone else is going out."[1]

JUSTIN TIMBERLAKE, SINGER

"Every relationship I've been in, I've overwhelmed the girl. They just can't handle all the love."[2]

MAHATMA GANDHI, ACTIVIST

"An eye for an eye makes the whole world blind."[3]

EMINEM, HIP-HOP ARTIST

"I want to raise my daughter the right way and not cut out on her like my father did to me."[4]

INTERVIEW

Subject: Pete Hughes, Soul Survivor leader

Soul Survivor: Why do you think ministry through action is so effective?

Pete Hughes: It communicates the heart of God to engage with the world He loves. The model of the Early Church in the book of Acts shows the effectiveness of proclamation and demonstration of the good news together. The good news was demonstrated by the generosity of the believers sharing with all those who had need. The hungry were fed, the lonely befriended, the sick were prayed for, and sinners found acceptance. It doesn't surprise me that the Lord added to [the] number [of believers] daily. The Church represented good news, and who wouldn't want to hear what they had to say. People began to listen because the Church had earned the right to speak into the hearts of those in the community. When people ask and are eager to hear about Jesus, evangelism becomes a lot less daunting and a lot more effective.

See the rest of this interview and more thought-provoking quotes at www.SoulSurvivorEncounter.com.

the story

As you work through this section, you may want to have the students alternate reading different parts, or summarize the themes yourself.

Love is everywhere, but what is it? Movies, books, songs and magazines are filled with ideas of love, and we see it portrayed on television all the time. Go to any airport where people are coming or going and you'll see love as people embrace, smile and say hello! So what is love? Is it passion, pride, sorrow, action? Pinning down one definition of love is not an easy thing to do.

SURVIVORS

Love is on display throughout the Bible and in history books as well. But the spiritual survivors profiled in this section, demonstrated love as compassion, kindness, loyalty or action. You might find that true love can be wilder and more powerful than you've ever imagined.

GOD IS LOVE

The Bible says "God is love" (1 John 4:8). But this doesn't mean that the words "love" and "God" can be used interchangeably. *God* is *love*, but *love* isn't *God* in the sense that *love* is an infinite, personal Being to be worshiped. Rather, love is at the center of God's nature and character. God is all about love.

It's easy to move quickly past John 3:16, particularly if you have students who have grown up in church. Yet the verse is packed with truth—take your time discussing it.

Action

Read John 3:16 and then answer the following questions as they relate to this verse: What do you think was God's motivation for sending Jesus to die for our sins? Who is God's love for? Is His love reserved for a certain group of people?

THE GOOD SAMARITAN

Many of us are familiar with the story of the good Samaritan—it is a parable Jesus told about a man who went out of his way to help somebody who was hurt. But the story of the good Samaritan shows love coming from the person from whom you would least expect it to come. In that day and age, Samaritans were looked down on and not well regarded by the Jews. Because of this, the story is an exceptional example of radical love and compassion.

Action

Read Luke 10:29-37. Why do you think the religious leader in this passage wanted to justify himself? Why do you think Jesus told him a story about such radical love? What is the story of the good Samaritan truly about?

The conversation between Christ and the religious leader in this passage is very significant. The leader asks what he must do to inherit eternal life, and the conversation becomes a showdown between grace and works. What's the connection between this passage and love? The story of the good Samaritan demonstrates a radical love for people that we are unable to produce through our own effort—it takes the power of the Holy Spirit working in us to love like that. The major point is that we can only find this love in God's grace.

THE LOYALTY OF RUTH

The book of Ruth is a great story. Ruth was from Moab, a country that didn't follow God. But when her husband died, Ruth made a decision to leave her country, move in with her mother-in-law, Naomi, and live in a country that followed God. The two women had no means of supporting themselves, but Ruth was determined to help Naomi and do what was right. She told her, "Don't urge me to leave you. . . . Where you go I will go and where you stay I will stay. Your people will be my people and your God my God" (Ruth 1:16).

Action

Now read Ruth 1–2. Do you think it was hard for Ruth to go with Naomi? Why did Boaz praise Ruth? How did Ruth's actions show love and loyalty?

Several passages in the book of Ruth can lead to a great discussion about whether love is a feeling or a choice. It is valuable for teenagers to grapple with love being something other than a feeling. Feelings can be truly part of love, but there are also many situations in life when love is a choice or a commitment—sometimes in addition to feelings. You might discuss this question: Was Ruth's love for Naomi a feeling or a choice?

LOVE IN ACTION

It is significant for young people to understand that love must contain action, not merely words. Harriet Tubman's life illustrates one form of love in action.

Harriet Tubman's life is a monument to courage and determination born out of love for people. Born into slavery in Maryland in the early 1800s, Harriet escaped and played a major role in freeing other slaves by helping coordinate the Underground Railroad—a secret network that transported escaped slaves to freedom in northern America and in Canada. Tubman risked great danger to herself but ended up freeing more than three hundred slaves.[5]

break it down

Complete the following activity individually.

Action

What do you think about love? In the space provided, write some examples of what true love looks like in your life and what true love does not look like in your life. Then circle the following situations that represent true love:

1. A girl at school seems to have a new boyfriend every week.
2. You let your younger brother watch cartoons on TV, even though you'd rather watch a basketball game.
3. You tell your friend you're so thankful she's in your life, but whenever she calls, you're too busy to talk.
4. Whenever you're around someone whom you consider a pretty close friend, he or she always points out what you're doing wrong.
5. Someone gently tells you something you've done wrong. It's never fun to hear criticism, but the person only talked to you about it because your actions were hurtful to someone else.

The point here is not to criticize others who have let us down but to apply concepts to real life. You might want to ask the students to also think about this question: Can a confrontation or constructive criticism be a form of true love?

comeback

Gather together in small groups and discuss the following questions. If you're working on this study alone, find a friend or relative with which to discuss your thoughts.

- What does it mean to truly love someone? What does it mean for someone to truly love you?
- Do you think love is more a feeling or a choice? What's the balance between the two?
- How can the concept of grace help you show love for someone you normally wouldn't show love for?
- Can you think of anyone you know who has demonstrated love for others and love for God? How has this person demonstrated this?

project revolution

Write down ideas for a project that you can complete outside the church walls this week. Read the suggestion in this section to help you get started.

BLESS YOUR TEACHERS

Set aside a day that you will dedicate to praying for your teachers. Remember, sometimes love is a feeling and sometimes love is a choice. After you have prayed for your teachers, choose at least three that you know or have had class with and give them each a note or a card thanking them for what they do. Then, at the end of the day, set aside a time when you pray that God would continue to bless all of your teachers. If you're doing this exercise during the summer, do the same exercise for parents, youth pastors, pastors or volunteer leaders in your youth group.

momentum

As the study comes to a close, encourage the students to read Scripture and pray on their own through the week. Reading the verses below is one option.

If you want to go further, check out the Time in the Word verses.

TIME IN THE WORD

Day 1—1 Corinthians 13
Day 2—Luke 6:31-35
Day 3—1 John 3:16-18
Day 4—1 John 5:1-2
Day 5—Deuteronomy 6:5; Leviticus 19:18

coming to a close

An important part of any small-group study is the time spent in prayer for one another. This can be done in several ways. Because this is the final session in this study, consider doing something special for your final prayer time. Lead the group in worship, serve Communion, or repeat a prayer method that worked well in previous sessions. Whatever you do, take some time to make a lasting impression on the students this week.

AFTER THE MEETING

1. **Evaluate:** Discuss the evening with your volunteer leaders and evaluate how God worked, what went well, what did not go well. You will also want to discuss with your leaders what study you'd like to pursue next—you can also check www.SoulSurvivorEncounter.com for more studies like this one.
2. **Encourage:** Continue to contact the students during the week via phone calls, notes, e-mails or instant messages.
3. **Equip:** Find a new study that you'd like to work on.
4. **Pray:** Continue to pray for the students and the next group gathering.
5. **Project Revolution:** Complete a project and discuss it with the students at the next group gathering.

FINAL SESSION NOTE

You've done a fantastic job caring for the students during this study. Take some time to rest and care for yourself before you start the next study.

Session One

1. Jim Bakker, quoted at *Bartleby.com*. http://www.bartleby.com/66/37/5237.html (accessed March 20, 2004).
2. Robert Levy, "Interview with Microsoft's .NET Compact Framework Technical Evangelist," *Devbuzz.com*. http://www.devbuzz.com/content/zinc_dotnet_compact_framework_tech_evangelist_pg1.asp (accessed March 20, 2004).
3. Mel Gibson, quoted at *American Clergy Leadership Conference*. http://www.aclc.info/quotes_mel_gibson-passion.htm (accessed June 25, 2004).
4. Mahatma Gandhi, quoted at *mkgandhi.org*. http://www.mkgandhi.org/epigrams/c.htm#Christ (accessed June 25, 2004).
5. *Merriam-Webster's Collegiate Dictionary*, 10th ed., s.v. "evangelism."

Session Two

1. Sandra Bullock, quoted at *AllStarz.org*. http://www.allstarz.org/sandra/quotes.htm (accessed April 12, 2004).
2. Martin Luther, quoted at *Lutherans Online*. http://www.lutheransonline.com/servlet/lo_ProcServ/dbpage=page&GID=01031013600972584326486620&PG=01032013600972932616888092 (accessed April 12, 2004).
3. Jenny Lange, "An Interview with Angelina Jolie," *Landmines in Africa*, 6.2 (August 2002). http://maic.jmu.edu/journal/6.2/notes/jennylange/jennylange.htm (accessed April 3, 2004).
4. Joan Baez, quoted at *Quote Me On It*. http://www.quotemeonit.com/relationships.html (accessed April 12, 2004).
5. Bruce Olson, "The Man Who Became an Ant," *thinkwow.com*. http://www.thinkwow.com/bruchko/the_man_who_became_an_ant.htm (accessed April 12, 2003).
6. *Online Latin Dictionary*, s.v. "carnis." http://www.24hourlatin.com/cgi-bin/latindict.pl (accessed August 9, 2004).
7. *The New Testament Greek Lexicon*, s.v. "phroneo." http://www.studylight.org/lex/grk/view.cgi?number=5426 (accessed August 9, 2004).

Session Three

1. Jim Trelease, quoted at "Storytelling Quotes," *aaronshep.com*. http://www.aaronshep.com/storytelling/quotes.html (accessed April 14, 2004).
2. Jimi Hendrix, quoted at *A to Z Quotes.com*. http://www.atozquotes.com/searchdb.asp (accessed June 29, 2004).
3. Robert Moss, quoted at "Storytelling Quotes," *aaronshep.com*. http://www.aaronshep.com/storytelling/quotes.html (accessed April 14, 2004).
4. Ursula K. LeGuin, quoted at "Storytelling Quotes," *aronshep.com*. http://www.aaronshep.com/storytelling/quotes .html (accessed April 14, 2004).
5. Toad the Wet Sprocket, *Stories I Tell*, Sony Music Entertainment Inc., B0000027JR, compact disc (*Fear*, 1991).

Session Four

1. Francis Beaumont, quoted at *BrainyQuote*. http://www.brainyquote.com/quotes/authors/f/francis_beaumont.html (accessed April 3, 2004).
2. Abraham Lincoln, quoted at *Creative Quotations*. http://www.creativequotations.com/cgi-bin/sql_search3.cgi?keyword=service&boolean=and&frank=all&field=all&database=all (accessed June 29, 2004).
3. Cathleen Falsani, "Bono's American Prayer," *Christianity Today*, March 2003. http://www.christianitytoday.com/ct/2003/003/2.38.html (accessed April 3, 2004).
4. Saint Francis of Assisi, quoted at *Creative Quotations*. http://www.creativequotations.com/cgibin/sql_search3.cgi?keyword=service&boolean=and&frank=all&field=all&database=all (accessed April 12, 2004).

Session Five

5. Mike Pilavachi, *The Urban Adventure* (Watford, England: Soul Survivor, 2001), p. 28.

Session Five

1. Marisha Rosenski, "Duvall: Josh Carter," *30music.com*. http://www.30music.com/int.php?int=44 (accessed April 18, 2004).
2. Andrew Cohen, "God Helps Those Who Help Themselves: An Interview with Evander Holyfield," *What is Enlightenment? Magazine*. http://www.wie.org/j15/holyfield.asp (accessed April 18, 2004).
3. Reza F. Safa, "Plant the Word of God in Their Hearts," *Beliefnet*. http://www.belief.net/story/109/story_10974_1.html (accessed April 18, 2004).
4. Mark Marvel, "Ramrodman," *Interview Magazine*, February 1997. http://www.findarticles.com/cf_dls/m1285/n2_v27/19192189/p1/article.jhtml (accessed April 18, 2004).
5. Linda T. Stonehocker, "Fold Zandura Interview," *The Phantom Tollbooth*, May 9, 1998. http://www.tollbooth.org/features/fz.html (accessed April 18, 2004).
6. James Strong, *Strong's Exhaustive Concordance of the Bible* (Nashville, TN: Thomas Nelson Publishers, 1978), #3875.

Session Six

1. Charles White, "Celebrity Interviews: Jennifer Knapp," *Christianity.com*. http://www.christianity.com/partner/Article_Display_Page/0,,PTID42281%7CCHID147904%7CCIID1761328,00.html (accessed April 26, 2004).
2. Dale Thompson, quoted at *Star-Interviews.com*. http://www.star-interviews.com/dalethompson-singer-of-for-bride.html (accessed April 26, 2004).
3. Jeff Gordon, quoted in David Caldwell, "Godspeed," *Beliefnet*. http://www.beliefnet.com/story/85/story_8550_1.html (accessed April 26, 2004).
4. Anthony Decurtis, "Marilyn Manson: The BeliefNet Interview," *Beliefnet*. http://www.beliefnet.com/story/78/story_7870_1.html (accessed April 26, 2004).
5. James Strong, *Strong's Exhaustive Concordance of the Bible* (Nashville, TN: Thomas Nelson Publishers, 1978), #2098.
6. C. S. Lewis, *The Screwtape Letters* (San Francisco, CA: HarperCollins Publishers, 2001), p. 69.

Session Seven

1. Clint Eastwood, quoted in *Reader's Digest*, April 2004, p. 73.
2. Dietrich Bonhoeffer, quoted at *CreativeQuotations*. http://www.creativequotations.com/cgi-bin/sql_search3.cgi?keyword=obedience&boolean=and&frank=all&field=all&database=all (accessed June 30, 2004).
3. Dr. Matthew Lukwiya, quoted in *Parade* (February 15, 2004), p. 15.
4. S. Rickly Christian, *Alive* (Grand Rapids, MI: Zondervan Publishing House, 1985), p. 162.

Session Eight

1. Dave Matthews, quoted in "Quotable Quotes," *Reader's Digest*, May 2004, p. 6.
2. Tom DeLonge, quoted in "To Quote," *Youthworker*, May/June 2003, p. 13.
3. Julian of Norwich, quoted in David Kopp, *Praying the Bible for Your life* (Colorado Springs, CO: WaterBrook Press, 1999), p. 37.
4. Jim Cymbala, *Fresh Wind, Fresh Fire* (Grand Rapids, MI: Zondervan Publishing House, 1997), p. 71.
5. Mark Price, "The Pickup Artist," *Charlotte.com*. http://www.contracostatimes.com/mld/observer/living/8127110.htm?1c (accessed June 30, 2004).
6. Mother Teresa, quoted at *The Nobel Prize Internet Archive*. http://www.almaz.com/nobel/peace/1979a.html (accessed June 30, 2004).

7. Mother Teresa, "Mother Teresa's Prayer," quoted at *Recovery Prayers.com*. http://recoveryprayers.homestead.com/prayer2.html (accessed June 30, 2004).

Session Nine

1. Alicia Keys, quoted at *Said What*. http://www.saidwhat.co.uk/quotes.php?name=Alica Keys& type=2 (accessed June 30, 2004).
2. Martin Luther, quoted at *SpiritualJunkFood.com*. http://www.spiritualjunkfood.com/quotable_quotes.htm (accessed June 30, 2004).
3. Saint Therese of Lisieux, quoted in Richard Foster, *Prayers from the Heart* (San Francisco, CA: HarperCollins Publishers, 1994), p. 47.
4. Bono, quoted in "People of the Year: Bono," interview by Anthony Bozza, *Rolling Stone.com*. http://www.rollingstone.com/news/story?id=5918448 (accessed June 30, 2004).

Session Ten

1. Chris Martin, quoted in *Rolling Stone*, April 15, 2004, p. 102.
2. J. Stephen Alessi, quoted in "To Quote," *Youthworker* (May/June 2002), p. 14.
3. Bob Briner, *Roaring Lambs* (Grand Rapids, MI: Zondervan Publishing House, 1993), p. 22.
4. Dean Batali, quoted in "To Quote," *Youthworker* (September/October 2002), p. 14.
5. Corrie ten Boom, *The Hiding Place* (New York: Bantam Books, 1984), p. 238.

Session Eleven

1. Wayne Gretzky, quoted at *GoodQuotes.com*. http://www.good quotes.com/celebrityquotes.htm (accessed June 30, 2004).
2. Brent Bradley, quoted at *SpiritualJunkFood.com*. http://www.spiritualjunkfood.com/quotable_quotes.html (accessed June 30, 2004).
3. Abraham Lincoln, quoted in S. Rickly Christian, *Alive!* (Grand Rapids, MI: Zondervan Publishing House, 1995), p. 195.
4. Brother David, *God's Smuggler to China* (Carol Stream, IL: Tyndale House, 1981), pp. 7-8.
5. "Humanimals: Wild Makeovers," *The Discovery Channel*, May 6, 2004. http://health.discovery.com/schedule/episode.jsp?episode=0&cpi=104091&gid=0&channel=DHC (accessed July 27, 2004).

Session Twelve

1. Dr. Phil McGraw, quoted in "Quotable Quotes," *Reader's Digest* (May 2004), p. 61.
2. Justin Timberlake, quoted at *GoodQuotes.com*. http://www.good quotes.com/celebrityquotes.htm (accessed July 6, 2004).
3. Mahatma Gandhi, quoted at *GoodQuotes.com*. http://www.good quotes.com/celebrityquotes.htm (accessed July 6, 2004).
4. Eminem, quoted in "To Quote," *Youthworker* (May/June 2003), p. 11.
5. "The Life of Harriet Tubman," *New York History Net*. http://www.nyhistory.com/harriettubman/life.htm (accessed July 6, 2004).